"Some say that prize fighting is the most thrilling of all sports. Cynics say it is 'the art of modified murder' . . . But say what you will — prize fighting has enriched sports literature with many of the strangest stories ever told."
See page vii . . . Punching with Bill Stern

BILL STERN'S
FAVORITE
BOXING
STORIES

Illustrated by
LOUIS GLANZMAN

POCKET BOOKS, INC., Rockefeller Center, N. Y.

BILL STERN'S FAVORITE BOXING STORIES

POCKET BOOK *edition published December,* 1948

1ST PRINTING ....NOVEMBER, 1948

A MAC DAVIS FEATURE

This POCKET BOOK is printed from
brand-new plates made from newly
set, large, clear, easy-to-read type.

CONTENTS *Round by Round*

PUNCHING
WITH BILL STERN

YOU ARE IN A RINGSIDE SEAT IN THE MOST FASCINATING sports-land of all—the boxing world!

Some say that prize fighting is the most thrilling of all sports. Some cynics say that prize fighting is "the art of modified murder." And some say that it is an ugly, brutal and swinish business. But say what you will—prize fighting has enriched sports literature with many of the strangest stories ever told—true tales far stranger than fiction.

Within the covers of this book I have tried to tell you some of these stories. I have tried to spin boxing yarns rarely heard and told, stories that never made the headlines and never show up in the musty record books.

Of those you are about to read, most are new and some are old, but to my way of thinking, all the stories in this book are richly flavored with romance, reveal something of the strange drama, fantastic legends, raw courage and rich humor of a land and people apart.

Give a little and take a little from memory sprinkled with resin dust. There goes the bell. No time left for further sparring. So grab yourself a ringside seat for an eyeful and earful of my favorite boxing stories.

BARE-KNUCKLE PUGS

The first modern prize fighter of whom there is any record is James Figg of England.

In his youth, a tough and illiterate husky, James Figg was a celebrated wrestler and swordsman. However, when he ran out of wrestling opponents, he turned to fighting with his fists. Thus, in 1716, bare-knuckle fighting made its official modern debut when James Figg proclaimed himself the heavyweight champion of the world. He was a ring marvel and he reigned as undisputed heavyweight champion until 1730, when at the age of 36, he retired from the ring—undefeated.

James Figg's style of fist fighting set a new fashion in the world of sports. Upon his retirement, he opened a school for teaching. His place was called "Figg's Academy for Boxing." His boxing school in London became the most popular spot in England, and men from all over the world went there to learn the art of "Figg's Fighting." That tough and illiterate bare-knuckle pug became the idol of England, and to his boxing academy came many of the most famous men of that time—Sir Robert Walpole, the Prime Minister of England, Alexander Pope, Dean Swift and others from all walks of life. When James Figg died at the age of 40, he left behind him a rich heritage, for Figg's style of fighting with bare knuckles spread throughout the world.

James Figg of England was the first of the great bare-knuckle champions. An American gentleman from Boston, John L. Sullivan, was the last bare-knuckle champion of the world. However, from James Figg to John L. Sullivan, there were other celebrated bare-knuckle boxing champions, fighters who made history.

For example, there is the story of a man who in his day won acclaim as a bare-knuckle champion, but that fact has been forgotten in the immeasurably greater fame he achieved in other fields.

He came from Virgina, the son of a well-to-do family. As a boy, husky and strong, he was handy with his dukes, and he loved a tough scrap. However, he had to do most of his bare-knuckle fighting in secret, for his family of cultured gentlemen and gentlewomen would have been horrified if he were discovered engaged in the brutal sport. But that boy from Virginia gained such a wide reputation in the fistic circles of his time, that when he was only sixteen years old, he was recognized as bare-knuckle boxing champion of Virginia.

All that happened a long time ago. His fame as a fist-fighter has been completely forgotten, but curiously enough, American history always will remember him as another kind of fighter, for he was the Father of Our Country and the first President of the United States— George Washington.

THERE ARE MORE ODD FACTS CONNECTED WITH THE CAREER of the old-time champion, Jem Mace, than with any other fighter in fistic history. To begin with, it is interesting to note that Mace, who began fighting about a hundred years ago, is responsible for most of the development of modern skill in the ring. He invented the left jab and taught it to a number of boxers in a school he ran in Australia. Among his pupils were such immortals of the ring as Peter Jackson, regarded as the greatest boxer ever seen in any squared circle, and a skinny red-haired blacksmith's helper named Bob Fitzsimmons.

Jem Mace began life as a wandering gypsy, became notorious as a pickpocket. In some manner, Mace fell in love with the violin and picked up a precarious living going from county fair to county fair, playing for pennies.

It was thanks to his fiddle that Jem Mace took his first step on his true career as a fighter. One day, before he had reached his eighteenth birthday, three drunken fishermen pounced on him, broke his violin over his head, and started to beat him up. Jem Mace shook himself loose and then proceeded to give the three men the beating of their lives. The fight was watched by an admiring rural circus promoter. When it was over he propositioned Jem, with the result that the young man with the handy fists became a prize fighter. He took on all comers in a circus boxing booth that travelled up and down England.

Although Jem Mace never weighed over 160 pounds, he fought his way up the ladder until he became heavyweight champion of the world, a title he richly deserved since he fought in almost every country in the world.

He was forty years old when he sailed to America for the first time. He met Tom Allen in New Orleans, and, after spotting his opponent more than ten years and over fifty pounds, defeated him for the world's heavyweight championship by a knockout.

Through all this Jem Mace never gave up his love for his violin. It went with him everywhere, which made for a lot of travelling because Mace fought in the ring for fifty-six years! The climax of his career came in South Africa where two well-known prize fighters were vying for the heavyweight championship. Mace fought both of these youngsters within the space of one week—and knocked them both cold! What's more, Jem Mace was seventy-one years old when he accomplished this feat!

When the gypsy pickpocket died at the ripe old age of eighty, he was mourned all over the world. And to the end, Jem Mace was true to both his arts. For he died clutching his violin with one hand, and a pair of boxing gloves with the other.

ONE OF THE MOST AMAZING FIGURES IN THE WORLD OF fistiana was John Morrissey, the obscure Bowery saloon bouncer who clawed and fought his way to the top of the heap—only to stumble and fall to the lowest depths after a meteoric career. A woman destroyed him.

Beginning as a green country boy who fought his bloody way from saloon brawls to pitched ring battles, John Morrissey hit the top in October, 1853, when he defeated James "Yankee" Sullivan for the heavyweight championship. Sullivan, who was not a Yankee but an Irishman, was a fugitive from English justice. The battle was staged on a farm meadow in the town of Boston Corner, Massachusetts. The purse was $1000 in gold and the title in dispute was the bare-knuckle heavyweight championship of the world.

A few days before the fight, the peaceful town was invaded by a strange army of hoodlums armed with pistols, knives, brass knuckles and brickbats. The police force of that little town took one look at the visitors and simply vanished from sight. Boston Corner became a no-man's land. To while away the dull hours before the fight, the band of ruffians amused themselves by slugging the honest citizens and robbing and pillaging their houses. Those of the visitors who did not feel like sleeping in barns merely took possession of the homes of the terrified inhabitants.

The fight took place on October 12th. It was a bloody

and bruising battle, as might have been expected. Sullivan clouted Morrissey at will, but the proud ex-saloon bouncer refused to go down. In the 37th round Morrissey finally went to his knees for the first time under Sullivan's ferocious attack. Unable to rise, the humbled champion called on his seconds for assistance. A horde of frenzied spectators rushed into the ring. A dozen fist fights broke out outside the ropes. At last, peace was restored. The crowd looked for the fight to resume. To everyone's astonishment, the referee made a startling announcement. He declared that Morrissey had won because James "Yankee" Sullivan had failed to toe the mark in time.

If there had been trouble before, it was nothing compared to what now followed. The supporters of the two fighters clashed in wild fury. Every possible weapon was used as the scene exploded into bloody battle. Back and forth, all through the formerly peaceful town, the struggle spread. Before order was restored, the Governor of the state had to be asked for help. Troops were despatched to the scene and quiet was restored at last.

That strange fight for the heavyweight title that almost destroyed a town, also doomed the two participants to misfortune. For "Yankee" Sullivan it meant a life of crime in California and a noose tightened around his neck by the San Francisco Vigilantes. For John Morrissey, another fate was in store, as inevitable as it was unexpected on that day in 1853.

It was a woman who brought Morrissey to his knees, a woman who belonged to another man.

About a year after winning what he called the "bare-knuckle heavyweight championship of the world" John Morrissey was riding on top of the world. His favorite haunt was the back room of Wallack's Theatre, in New York. One night, surrounded by his cronies and hangers-on, a mischievous gleam came into John Morrissey's eye.

The evening had been a bore and the champion, craving excitement, had suddenly thought of something.

"I want some fun!" he shouted, pounding the table before him with a huge fist. "And 'tis only a fight that will give it to me!" He clapped a heavy hand on the shoulder of one of his henchmen, a tough, bruising middleweight fighter of wide repute. "You," continued the champion, "you, Tony Cassitty will fight Andy Mallon of Tom Hyer's camp and I'll personally bet $100 on the side that you win. You all know how I hate that Tom Hyer and this will give me a chance to see one of his fighters beaten up. I'll send the challenge this very minute!"

The crowd around the champion murmured approval. Everyone knew that Hyer was Morrissey's bitter rival both in business and in politics. The match was quickly arranged for a purse of $100.

There was only one person who felt some concern about the match. This was Sally Minturn, sweetheart of Andy Mallon. She pleaded with Andy to call off the fight. "Please, Andy," she begged. "You mustn't fight Cassitty. He's so much bigger than you are and stronger. I've got a feeling about this fight, Andy. Call it a premonition if you like."

Andy Mallon laughed at Sally's fears. Throwing his arm around her waist, he said, "It's a fine New Year's you and I will be spending with the hundred dollars I'm going to win! And won't that John Morrissey be sore!"

Boxing was illegal in New York in those days. The match was fought in a clearing in the woods before a small audience of fight fans who were in-the-know. John Morrissey, at ringside, was having the time of his life. Round after round went by as Cassitty unmercifully beat the lighter Mallon to a pulp. But the Hyer man refused to quit. Had Morrissey not sneered and taunted him, it is possible that Sally Minturn's sweetheart might have given up the struggle. But the insults only spurred the lighter man. Sheer courage and stubbornness carried Andy Mallon into the 99th round. It was as far as he could go. In that round Cassitty delivered a crushing blow and Mallon sank in a heap. It didn't take long to see that the beaten man would never move again. He was dead.

When Sally Minturn heard the news of her sweetheart's death, she went looking for John Morrissey. It was New Year's Eve that she finally found him, celebrating the holiday at his favorite bar. Gun in hand, the girl pushed her way through the crowd of revellers and faced the champion. Raising the gun, she aimed carefully and pulled the trigger before the paralyzed bystanders could raise a finger. There was only the sound of a click. The gun had jammed. John Morrissey snatched the weapon from the girl and laughed.

The grief-stricken girl drew back her lips. "I'm going to have my revenge, John Morrissey," she whispered viciously. "I've lost my Andy and it's your fault. I'll haunt you, John Morrissey, for the rest of your life!"

Again Morrissey laughed and turned away. In a few moments he had forgotten the incident completely. The girl was hustled out of the place and the New Year revels went on unabated. It seemed that nothing had happened to mar the occasion.

Nevertheless, things began to happen to John Morrissey. Challenged to a fight for his title by Bill Poole, Morrissey accepted and received one of the worst beatings of his career. His title was saved for him only through the prompt intervention of his henchmen who broke into the ring and brought the fight to an abrupt halt while the champion lay groveling in the dust.

Later, Morrissey discovered that a mysterious woman had staked Poole and had been behind his challenge. And when John Heenan began to plague Morrissey for a chance at the title, Morrissey decided to quit the ring rather than take the chance of meeting the challenger. Again, Morrissey learned that a mysterious woman was behind the Heenan challenge.

After retiring from the ring, John Morrissey became involved in politics. In a short time John Morrissey was a power to be reckoned with.

Meanwhile, unknown to Morrissey, beautiful Sally Minturn had become a famous Broadway musical star. The oath of revenge she had taken had never been forgotten. John Morrissey was elected to Congress. When he arrived in Washington he was snubbed and even derided by members of his own party. He was glad, at last, to slink back to New York and his old familiar haunts. Again, a mysterious woman's influence was found to be the cause of his downfall.

No sooner was he back in New York than John Morrissey became involved in serious trouble as a result of the exposé of the infamous Tweed Ring that was holding the city in a tight and crooked grip. Once again, a mysterious woman's influence lay behind John Morrissey's difficulties.

To forget his troubles, Morrissey went to Saratoga Springs. He built the famous race track that now stands there. Just as he was about to reap the fruits of his labors, the track was snatched from his grasp. John Morrissey was left penniless. And once again, as usual, a mysterious woman was behind it.

Disgraced, penniless, almost forgotten at the age of 47, John Morrissey died a broken-hearted man. Even the skies wept at his misery for the day of his funeral was a wild and stormy one. And the legend goes that as the grave-diggers shoveled wet earth upon his coffin, a veiled mysterious woman who stood at the edge of the little crowd around the grave was overheard to murmur, "Andy, at last John

Morrissey is dead. Rest in peace now, Andy. I've had my revenge."

THE FIRST PUGILIST TO HOBNOB WITH ARISTOCRACY ON equal terms was John "Gentleman" Jackson of England. Even more of a dandy than Gentleman Jim Corbett, was that old-time English champion among the bare knuckle heavyweights. John Jackson was a first-rate two-fisted man in the ring—a dignified and well-mannered gentleman out of it. In his scarlet coat and lace ruffles, Gentleman Jack was the center of attraction wherever he went. His famous school for boxing in London was the meeting place for the aristocrats and fashionable young men of his day, and even the King of England did not think it beneath him to visit the great fighter in his rooms.

Although boxing history best remembers Gentleman John Jackson as the man who licked Daniel Mendoza, the first Jewish champion, to win the heavyweight title in an era of great fighters, there is an interesting story connected with this old-time bare-knuckle hero that is little known. It's the tale of a man he discouraged from becoming a fighter.

One day a youth with a beautiful face and excellent physique came to Gentleman Jack's school for boxing lessons. The young man tried hard to become a fighter and Gentleman Jack spared no effort to develop his promising ability, but the odds were against the pupil. For the young fellow was a cripple.

Gentleman Jack and the young man became good friends and in time the famous bare knuckle champion persuaded his pupil to forsake his ambition to become a fighter, and seek fame elsewhere. So, the young man with the beautiful face became one of the world's immortal poets. His name was Lord Byron.

STOP THE FIGHT!

It was back in the '90s that the stirring episode in the history of the South known as "The War of Waycross" took place in the sovereign state of Georgia. Like the Trojan War of ancient times, this war, too, was started by a woman. But, unlike that bloody and bitter clash, this particular struggle was fought merely to repel an invasion of two prize fighters.

It all began one fine Sunday morning when the gallant, bearded William J. Northen, Governor of Georgia, was invited by a certain gracious lady to hear a sermon to be delivered at the Baptist Tabernacle by Dr. Len Broughton. Governor Northen accepted the invitation and escorted the gentle lady to the scene of the event that was to precipitate so memorable an affair.

Dr. Broughton's sermon was a bitter attack on the brutal and vulgar sport of prize fighting. So eloquent and fiery was the oration that all who heard it sat as though spellbound. Then, at its close, the sermon really rose to great heights.

"And what is more," thundered Dr. Broughton, "at this very moment two prize fighters, Jim Corbett, who calls himself heavyweight champion of the world, and Charlie Mitchell, so-called heavyweight champion of England, stand poised somewhere in our neighboring state of Florida waiting for an opportunity to cross into Georgia to stage a fight for the titles they hold! Imagine! A prize fight in our own state! Shall we tolerate such a brutal exhibition? Shall we permit the fair name of Georgia to be besmirched by two half-naked men pounding each other with fists? What are we going to do about it?"

Dr. Broughton stepped down with these words and strode from the Tabernacle. Cries of indignation rose from the audience. The gracious lady, tears in her eyes, turned to the Governor and said tremulously, "What can you do about this terrible thing?"

"Ma'am," replied the gallant Georgian, "This means only one thing—war!"

And war it was. Governor Northen, true to his word, went into action immediately. He issued an order alerting the State troops. He set guards at the borders of the state, and directed all trains entering Georgia be stopped. He then summoned his adjutant-general and other members of his staff, ordered a special troop train to be made ready. To the coastal towns of Georgia went the peremptory command to arm their companies and send them forthwith to Waycross. And, under the title of "Governor of Georgia and Commander-in-Chief of the Army and Navy of Georgia," Northen himself, determined to lead his troops personally against the invasion, thundered into Waycross and set up field headquarters!

To the boys and girls of Waycross all this was a picnic. The girls especially went wild with delight at the sight of all the handsome soldiers in their fine uniforms, white cross belts, plumes, sashes and gauntlets. In, fact, so impressed were they by the gallant lads that Governor Northen, grimly occupied in making plans to repel the coming invasion, found himself up to his neck in the screaming complaints from a delegation of angry and frantic mothers who bore down on him with the information that their daughters had blithely run away to get married to some of his soldiers!

At this very moment several panting scouts brought word

to the Governor's field headquarters that Jim Corbett and Charlie Mitchell, the two prize fighters, were about to attempt an entry into Georgia at a point on the St. Mary's River below Folkston. The delegation of mothers was eased out of the Governor's presence. And the Georgia Navy went into action!

Skiffs and flatboats, packed to the gunwales began to patrol the river. A cry of alarm went up. The little fleet had caught sight of a boatload of men bearing down on them. Guns were cocked. Then a cry went up from the approaching vessel. "Don't shoot! It's the Navy of Georgia with the Admiral aboard!" Quiet was restored. There was no bloodshed.

Meanwhile, Governor Northen held counsels of war with the assembled sheriffs of Charlton, Camden, Glynn, McIntosh, and Liberty Counties. As a result, one sheriff with a squad of soldiers was posted at the St. Mary's River. At points two miles apart on the railroad line, a sheriff and a squad of soldiers were installed. The Waycross Rifles and the Hussars, in a specially chartered troop train guarded forty miles of railroad, while the Brunswick Light Horse Guard took charge of forty miles in Camden County. And, to top it all, the Governor sent "spies" to Jacksonville to follow the movements of the "enemy"—the two prize fighters, Corbett and Mitchell.

In Jacksonville, Jim Corbett and Charlie Mitchell and their followers watched these preparations with open mouths. There was a hurried conference. The result was that the invaders decided not to invade. The Governor of Georgia won the War of Waycross without firing a shot. The fight between Corbett and Mitchell was fought right in Jacksonville. Corbett stopped Mitchell in three rounds.

It was only when the fight was over that the gallant and patriotic Governor Northen proclaimed the end of the war. The troops were sent home. The state of Georgia went back to its peaceful life, its fair name unsullied, its honor un-besmirched. The War of Waycross had been fought and won, the invasion of two prize fighters had been prevented. A toast to that gracious fair lady who had saved the honor of a great state!

NOWADAYS, AN IMPORTANT HEAVYWEIGHT BOXING BOUT IS A million dollar spectacle that attracts national attention, and the presence of some seventy-five thousand spectators from all walks of life. But it was not always thus.

More than half-a-century ago, two heavyweights fought a ring battle which lasted less than three minutes. A company of Texas Rangers and the soldiers of two countries tried to prevent that heavyweight prize fight from being staged.

Way back in 1896, when Jim Corbett was heavyweight champion of the world, the middleweight title was held by the Australian blacksmith, Ruby Robert Fitzsimmons. Fitz, who had held his title for five years, yearned for a crack at the big crown held by Gentleman Jim. In his way stood the broad shoulders of a ponderous heavyweight named Peter Maher who also had designs on the heavyweight championship. Maher ridiculed Ruby Bob and threatened to knock the Australian's block off any time he was brave enough to step into a ring with him to settle the issue.

While Fitz may have looked like a freak with his thin waist, long legs and powerful arms and shoulders, he was hardly the fighter to duck any man alive, no matter how big he was. It was easy for an enterprising promoter to match the two men. The fight was set to take place at Langtry, Texas, on the afternoon of February 21, 1896.

As soon as the match was set, things began to happen that made the Fitzsimmons-Maher encounter one of the oddities of fistic history. To begin with, prize fighting was against the law in the territories of the West, including Texas. As soon as the State officials got wind of the impending fight, a neat little surprise was arranged for the contestants. A company of fast-shooting, hard-riding Texas Rangers was dispatched posthaste to prevent the battle.

At the same time the Federal authorities were not to be caught napping either. The armed forces stationed in New Mexico and Arizona were ordered to march to the scene under instructions to stop the fight even if they had to resort to the use of arms.

With two armies converging on him, the foxy promoter, in turn, arranged a little surprise for the enemy. He quickly selected a new site for the contest. To evade the law of the United States, he found a small strip of land midway between Texas and Mexico along the Rio Grande River.

When the Texas Rangers and the United States Army arrived, they were stumped. The battleground was now on Mexican territory. The ring was pitched in a circus tent and the handful of spectators were obliged to walk across a little bridge some five hundred yards from El Paso, Texas. The Federals and the Rangers, aimlessly toying with their loaded weapons, had nothing to do but assemble on a high hill overlooking the ring and watch the fight.

Peter Maher climbed through the ropes, blustering and bragging. "Where's that skinny freak?" he roared. "I'll break him in half!"

Bob Fitzsimmons, powerful shoulders, freckles, spindly legs and all, crawled into the ring, cool as a cucumber, an amused smile on his lips.

As the referee called the two fighters for instructions, word was brought to the contestants that the Mexican government had dispatched soldiers to drive the Americanos off Mexican territory.

There was no time to figure a way out of this new difficulty. The bell rang for the fight to begin. Maher made a wild lunge at the elusive and tricky Fitzsimmons. Just as the men made their first contact, the promoter of the bout stuck his head through the ropes and shouted, "Make it quick, boys! The Mexican Army is on its way here to stop the fight!"

When Bob Fitzsimmons heard this, he decided that he would have to work fast. With fists flying, he sailed into the lumbering heavyweight who stood between him and a chance at the title. After two minutes of inflicting the most terrible punishment on his adversary's face and body, Fitz dropped Peter Maher to the canvas, out cold. Then, quickly, he helped Maher's handlers revive the fallen gladiator, and the two fighters, the promoter, and the handful of spectators took to their heels towards the little bridge to El Paso and American territory. They were thundering across the boundary between the two countries just as the Mexican soldiers hove into view, shooting their rifles into the air. In a spot like this, American stood with American. The United States officers of the law did not interfere with the sorely pressed fighters and spectators, permitting them to board a waiting train.

Thus, ended one of the strangest heavyweight fights in history—a ring-battle that is now merely a line in the musty record-books, reading: "Bob Fitzsimmons knocked out Peter Maher in one round on February 21, 1896." But behind that one line lies hidden a fantastic story of a heavyweight prize fight which lasted less than three minutes, yet a whole company of Texas Rangers and the soldiers of two countries tried to stop it.

DRINK UP, GENTLEMEN

It is difficult to believe that France, which has turned out such rugged fistic warriors as Eugene Criqui, Marcel Thil, Georges Carpentier and Marcel Cerdan, hardly knew what a good fighter looked like until some forty years ago.

Willie Lewis, a handsome baby-faced soft-spoken American dandy came to France in 1909 to ply his wares and became the darling of the Parisian boulevards. Everywhere he went tremendous crowds flocked to see him and in every café he was the subject of animated conversation. Lewis made a tremendous impression on the Parisians who were surprised to note his fine manners and soft voice, so unlike what they expected to see in a prize fighter.

One afternoon, on a day that Lewis was supposed to fight, he decided to take a walk on the boulevards for some relaxation. It chanced that several gay Frenchmen who were rabid fight fans recognized the famous American and promptly invited him to join them on a merry tour of the town. When they stopped in one of the big cafés, somebody ordered a round of drinks. Lewis, who never touched liquor, at first refused to partake of the refreshments, but was finally persuaded to try a little absinthe. Not being a drinking man, Willie Lewis did not know that the innocent-looking pale green drink had a terrific kick. He gulped down about a dozen shots of the stuff.

How he found his way back to the arena that night was forever a mystery to Willie Lewis. When he did come to a little, it was to find himself in his dressing room getting into his fighting togs. His manager and handlers were so excited about the coming bout that they failed to observe that their fighter was just short of being completely pie-eyed.

At some point in the evening, Lewis found himself in the center of the ring trying to listen to the referee, but not hearing a word of what the man was saying. A moment later, the bell clanged.

Instead of squaring off against his opponent, the stupe-fied Lewis walked over to the referee, shook hands with him, and promptly knocked that innocent bystander cold with a well-directed punch to the whiskers. The jammed arena howled with surprise. In the midst of the uproar the luckless referee was dragged out of the ring and another official was quickly substituted.

The change made no difference to the befuddled Lewis. Round after round saw the American stalking the poor referee from pillar to post and throwing punches at him from all directions. The thoroughly frightened man ran all over the ring, from corner to corner, ducking the blows as best he could, and shouting at the top of his voice "No! No, monsieur! I am not ze man you are fighting! Zere is ze man you want to hit! I am ze referee, voyons! Stop! Oh, mon Dieu, zis crazee American is trying to kill me!"

To which the American, peering through bloodshot and half-glazed eyes, would only growl, "Come on, Frenchie! Let's give the people a show! Put up your fists and fight!"

Needless to relate, the crowd roared with laughter as the embattled referee raced all over the ring trying to avoid Willie Lewis' dynamite-laden fists. No one was happier when the final bell rang than this poor man in the middle.

As for Willie Lewis, it was well into the next day, after a long and dreamless night's sleep, before he discovered that he had come close to murdering two innocent referees who were guilty of nothing more than trying to do their jobs. It's pretty certain that the American who introduced the sport of boxing to la belle France never touched inno-cent-looking absinthe again.

IF YOU KNOW YOUR BOXING HISTORY THEN YOU SURELY know the fame of the great John L. Sullivan, the Boston Strong Boy, who won himself imperishable glory as the first of the world's modern heavyweight champions. In his day, Sullivan was a magnificent fighter, perhaps the great-est of them all. His skill is legendary. It is not better known, though, than his penchant for high living and wild drinking sprees. No man could stand up with John L. when it came to bending the elbow. Throughout his slash-ing career the Boston terror cut a wide swathe of high jinks. And then, suddenly, Sullivan went on the water wagon, never to take another drink. For fifteen years, till the day he died, Sullivan lived an exemplary life.

What was it that made John L. Sullivan suddenly change from a two-fisted, roaring drinker to a sober and gentle man? The story behind the conversion was for a long time unknown.

In his cups, Sullivan was a sight to make brave men flinch and shudder in their boots. Only children, the news-boys and the bootblacks, loved the great John L. with an adoration that would admit no flaw in the champion.

After wading through champagne to the tune of a mil-lion dollars, Sullivan opened a gaudy tavern in the heart of New York. Noble as were his intentions, Sullivan paid little attention to business. He continued to go from bar to bar followed by his legion of admiring fans, drinking in his own fabulous way, and having himself a grand and gay time.

Then, one day, the rent fell due for his tavern. It was a little matter of two hundred dollars. John L. searched his pockets, checked the cash on hand, then looked up in wonder. At last he was flat broke, not a dime to his name.

However, there were still his faithful friends to call upon for help and Sullivan sent a messenger to one of the best of them, a chap named George Considine. "Tell him I've got to have it," said Sullivan. "And bring it back right away. Go on now!"

When Considine received the message from Sullivan he refused point blank. "Nothing doing!" he roared. "I won't give Sullivan two hundred cents! He'll only go on one of his tears and drink it up! Tell him that!"

When the messenger returned with the news Sullivan was dumbfounded. Surely a good friend wouldn't refuse him so small a matter as two hundred dollars for rent! With a slightly watery look in his black eyes, Sullivan sent the messenger off again, to another of his good friends. Again the messenger returned empty-handed.

John L. Sullivan's eyes slowly filled with unbidden tears and his great head sank on his chest. "Two of my best friends," he murmured, his booming voice strangely subdued, "two of my very best friends and they turn me down for a paltry loan of two hundred dollars because they think I'll use it for drink. Ah, it's like two daggers being driven into me heart!" The great champion shook his mighty head. "Maybe they're right. Maybe the great John L. is no longer trustworthy for a mere two hundred dollars. Maybe I have lived a wild and reckless life." His head lifted and the words rang out. "But I promise now that I'll never take another drink the longest day I live!"

John L. Sullivan never broke his vow. For fifteen years he rode the water wagon. What is more, to the day he died he travelled up and down the country preaching to the youth of the land about the folly and evil of drink.

To TELL THE COMPLETE STORY OF THE CAREER OF HARRY Greb—in the opinion of many the greatest fighter pound for pound in boxing history—is almost impossible. Here was a man who never weighed over 160 pounds, was blind in one eye, and met everyone from middleweight to heavyweight. He beat Gene Tunney in the ring and Jack Dempsey in the training camp, lived high, wide and handsome, never trained for a fight, and yet lost a bare six times in over three hundred bouts! The incredible saga of this great fighter might best be explained by the story of his fight with Mickey Walker and all the things that happened in connection with it.

When Harry Greb was middleweight champion of the world, Mickey Walker, the Toy Bulldog, held the welterweight title. Walker's manager was the wily Jack Kearns, a man who always had great ambitions for his fighters. He sought a match for his man with Greb for the middleweight crown. Greb, who feared no one, gladly obliged, and the deal was made, the fight to be held in the Polo Grounds.

When Greb arrived in New York to set up his training camp for the fight, he was as big as a balloon, weighing some 180 pounds. Although he laughed at his worried friends and insisted that he would make the weight for the fight, Kearns and Walker were hugely pleased about the Human Windmill's poor condition. As the days passed, word got around that Greb was spending most of his time along the Great White Way.

On the night before the big fight, Jack Kearns, Walker's manager, went strolling down Broadway. What was his surprise—and pleasure—to see coming out of a gay night club the staggering and pie-eyed Harry Greb, a beauteous blonde hanging on each arm!

This was enough for Kearns and the smart money boys. Everyone rushed to bet his bankroll on Mickey Walker to win. Had they not been so hasty, they would have seen a strange sight.

As soon as Greb and the two blondes had ducked around the nearest corner, Harry's drunkenness disappeared. With a word of thanks, he dismissed the two girls who quickly vanished into the darkness. Then, cold sober and with a smile on his lips, Harry Greb went home to bed, his clever little masquerade having worked perfectly. All the bets sought by the smart money boys were snapped up by Greb's friends. It was the greatest sucker trap in boxing history and the smart boys fell for it, hook, line and sinker.

Then came the fight. Harry Greb was never greater. He gave Mickey Walker, a champion in his own right, a savage beating. It was only Mickey's game heart and Harry Greb's sentiment that saved the welterweight title-holder from a knockout in the final round. Crying, bleeding and battered, Mickey Walker was led back to his dressing room, convinced that Harry Greb was unbeatable. The smart gamblers were cleaned to the bone. Greb made himself a tidy little fortune by his clever masquerade.

Later that evening, the two men met again, but this time it was in a night club where the fighters had gone, each with his own party, to relax and have a good time. Someone told Walker that Greb was in the club, and he got up to join his recent adversary for a few drinks in friendly fashion. The two men got to talking, and their parties, disgusted at having been abandoned, went off.

Hours later, the two men were gently ushered to the sidewalk when the club closed for the night. Arm in arm they walked down the street on the way to visit some friends. As they reached the door of the house they were about to enter, Mickey Walker turned to Harry Greb and said, "You know, Harry, you Dutch so-and-so, I'd a licked you tonight if you hadn't stuck your thumb in my eye!"

Harry Greb flushed with anger. "Why, you Irish thus-

and-so, you may be a Toy Bulldog to some, but you're only a poodle to me!"

·With this exchange of politeness, the two men waded into each other hammer and tongs. For several minutes a bitter and bloody battle was silently fought between two fighters who, only hours before, had mixed it before thousands—and for plenty of dough!

"Here, and what's the meanin' o' this?" shouted a voice. And with those words, a big policeman grabbed each man by the scruff of the neck and pulled them apart. "Sure, and ye've fought enough, I'll be thinkin'." Hauling the two men along on either side of him, the cop flung first one, then the other, into a couple of taxicabs that stood at the curb. "Take 'em home!" cried the cop. "Let 'em sleep it off!"

It was barely a year later that Harry Greb's death on the operating table shocked the world of sport fans. How great a fighter he was in his heyday can be indicated by a remark once made by Mickey Walker years after those two memorable fights he had with the Human Windmill. "We became good pals after those fights," said Mickey, "and Harry and I stayed pals till the day he died."

"How do you think he would do against today's middle-weights?" someone asked the Toy Bulldog.

"Are you kidding?" asked Walker. "He could take care of most of our heavyweights!"

IT IS NOT GENERALLY KNOWN THAT TWO OF OUR MOST POPU-lar songs owe their origin to the sport of boxing. The next time you sing them with your favorite barber shop quartet, remember to give credit where it belongs.

The first song was born in a little place called Old Town, Louisiana. A company of strolling minstrels arrived one day to put on a performance in the local op'ry house.

To their chagrin, the visiting troubadors discovered that on the very same night a prize fight had been scheduled between two well-known local pugilists. To assure themselves of an audience, the enterprising minstrel men plastered the town's walls with placards promising a hot time in Old Town!

Intrigued by the signs, the local citizens forgot all about the prize fight and turned out to welcome the visiting troupe. In appreciation for the reception, a new melody was hastily prepared as the opening number. The song was called, naturally, "A Hot Time in the Old Town." When the Spanish-American War broke out, the song was adopted by our soldiers as their very own. It became, as well, the theme song of President Theodore Roosevelt, and was played wherever he went.

The second song was written some fifty years ago by Harry Armstrong, sparring partner of John L. Sullivan, himself. The training camp of that great champion was a gay and convivial place, for the mighty John L. was a wonderful host to all his friends and associates. One day, following a particularly joyous celebration, Harry Armstrong sat down to write a sentimental song to express his feelings. The song has since become the very heart and soul of quartet repertory. Its name? "Sweet Adeline." Give us a chord, Professor!

You might think it impossible to find an amusing story connected with the beetle-browed and humorless Max Schmeling, champion of the world by a sit-down strike. It can be done, though:

In 1938, Max Schmeling came back to America from Germany to meet Joe Louis for the second time. Schmeling's manager was the colorful little Jewish guy with the big cigar, known up and down Cauliflower Alley as Joe "Yussel" Jacobs.

"Der Maxie" brought with him from the homeland, Germany's leading sports announcer, a Nazi character named Arno Hellmiss, who was scheduled to broadcast the fight for the German sport fans by short wave from ringside.

Arno Hellmiss was as conceited, arrogant and boorish an individual as anyone had ever seen. He practically demanded that the people he came in contact with grovel at his well-shod feet. Naturally, the American reporters took a violent dislike to Hellmiss after running into him at Schmeling's training camp. They took turns at restraining each other from taking a poke at him.

On his own account, Hellmiss took a violent dislike to Schmeling's Jewish manager, Yussel Jacobs. On no occasion that offered did the German overlook the opportunity of belittling the little guy. Jacobs, however, returned kindness and consideration for the insults that were heaped on his head. The local reporters could not understand Jacobs' attitude.

"Why don't you take a poke at that Nazi bum?" they asked him. "You don't have to take that from him. Go on, we'll back you up!"

"No, fellers," little Yussel Jacobs would answer with a grin, "I wouldn't harm a hair on his head!"

Came the night of the fight, as everyone remembers, and Joe Louis handed Schmeling one of the most humiliating defeats in boxing history—a knockout in less time than had ever before been recorded in such a match. Hellmiss, who was at ringside for his broadcast, was so infuriated by this blow to the "superman" from Germany that he rushed away from the scene intent on drowning his sorrows before dashing off to take his boat home.

In some way Hellmiss found himself with Yussel Jacobs as his drinking partner at a bar not far from the docks.

The German took one drink and proceeded to get violently ill. Despised and shunned as he was by most people around him, Hellmiss found himself completely ignored—except by Joe Jacobs. It was the little Jewish manager who tenderly helped Hellmiss to the ship he was to sail on, undressed him with kind hands, put him to bed, and soothed the suffering broadcaster. The sick man continued to moan that he was dying. When his wails became too loud to stand, Jacobs called a doctor to examine the man.

The examination was brief. When it was over the doctor informed Jacobs that Hellmiss had been given a Mickey Finn and that nothing else was the matter with him. (A Mickey Finn, good reader, is a comparatively harmless little pill that is added to a drink in order to knock out the drinker. It is usually given to someone who is getting difficult to handle.)

Even a character like Arno Hellmiss could see clearly enough that he owed some gratitude to a man who helped him as much as Joe Jacobs was doing. When he could talk he said, "Joe, please forgive me. I've been rotten to you and you're the only one who helped me. Honest, Joe, I'm sorry for everything."

"Forget it, pal," answered the accommodating Jacobs. "We're all even now. Glad to do anything I can for a sick friend."

When the all-ashore signal was given, Joe Jacobs left the ship, but not till Hellmiss had bid him a tearful fond farewell, vowing again and again that he felt like a heel for the way in which he had acted.

At the foot of the gangplank, Joe was met by several angry friends. News of Jacobs' friendly activity in behalf of so hated a character as Hellmiss had gotten around quickly.

"What's the matter, Yussel?" demanded one of them.

"Have you gone nuts? What's the idea, helping that no-good bum after the way he treated you?"

"Wait a minute," said another pal, looking closely at little Joe, "I think maybe I smell around here a mouse. Could it be that you, Yussel, slipped this nasty character a Mickey Finn?"

"What are you talking about, a Mickey Finn?" demanded the indignant Joe Jacobs. "I should give a guy one Mickey Finn? I liked that fellow, Hellmiss. You think I'm a piker? I gave him *three* Mickey Finns!"

I'LL TELL THE WORLD

Nowadays the reporter covering an important prize fight works under the most favorable conditions, sitting close under the ring with a telegraph operator at his elbow to send out his running report as quickly as it is written. It wasn't always like that. There was a time in the history of boxing when a fight-reporter had to scramble to get his story to the public within a reasonable time. That is, if he got the story at all.

On a hot July afternoon in 1889, the immortal John L. Sullivan climbed into the ring to defend his heavyweight crown against his most dangerous challenger, Jake Kilrain. This title battle, the last world's championship match fought with bare knuckles, took place in a ring staked out on the turf at Richburg, Mississippi.

Although the Sullivan-Kilrain encounter was an important and historic one, there were only a few spectators. Prize fighting at the time was outlawed. Though most of the world knew this match was taking place, it had to be held virtually in secret.

The Governor of Mississippi had ordered the militia to the state borders to keep the fight mob from entering. While a number of reporters did manage to get to ringside, they learned with a shock that it would be impossible for them to send out their stories over the telegraph wires. The railroad, which controlled the wires, refused to let the reporters have access to them.

Among the writers was one, slightly more ingenious than the rest, named George Dickinson, covering the match for the old New York *World*. He knew that there was going to be trouble and he came prepared to get his story through.

George carried a bag of small rubber balls with him when he showed up at ringside. To the questions of his neighboring newsman he turned a deaf ear. He let them laugh all they pleased. When the fight started and the others saw what George was up to, the laugh was on the other side of their faces.

What George Dickinson did, as the fight went on, was scribble his running story on small slips of paper. As soon as he filled the slip he pushed it into a slit cut into a rubber ball. Every couple of rounds, he dashed back to the barricade that closed in the crowd, signalled to an assistant outside, and tossed him the balls crammed full of notes. The confederate leaped to the back of a horse, and dashed off a couple of miles where another man, a friendly telegraph operator, ripped open the balls, and sent out the story. Meanwhile the horseman was speeding back to the barricade to get the next batch of messages from Dickinson.

The fight, a bloody and brutal battle, went seventy-six rounds before it was stopped by the referee at the insistence of a doctor who warned that Kilrain would be killed if he continued. As soon as the fight was over—two hours and sixteen minutes after it had begun—the reporters at ringside dashed to catch a train that would take them far enough to reach a telegraph office that would accept their stories. Their haste was in vain. The complete story of the heavyweight title bout was already on the first page of the New York *World*. Just a bunch of innocent-looking rubber balls had made all the difference.

TODAY, ON THE OCCASION OF A BIG FIGHT FOR A WORLD'S title, millions of people all over the country cluster around their radios to listen to the blow-by-blow description of the contest. But did you ever wonder how nationwide radio broadcasting began? Not only is the story an interesting one, but there is also the fact that it is told against a background of sports.

It started back in 1921 with a man named Andy White. White was obsessed with the idea of presenting one radio program that could be heard at the same time all over the country. In those years, the idea was a fantastic one since there were only a handful of broadcasting stations. However, Andy White was determined to carry out his plan.

To begin with, White shopped around to find one radio program of such great interest that people everywhere would want to hear it. At last he found what he was looking for. It was a prize fight to be held on July 4, 1921, the heavyweight championship bout between the immortal Jack Dempsey, title-holder, and the glamorous Frenchman, Georges Carpentier. This international contest had captured the imagination of everyone in the world, and was to go down in history as the first prize fight to draw a gate of one million dollars.

Andy White went to see the man who was putting on the bout, Tex Rickard, at the time the greatest boxing promoter in the world. He asked Rickard's permission to sit at ringside and broadcast the fight to people throughout the United States.

The famous promoter ridiculed the idea. He pointed out to the ambitious Andy White that there was no broadcasting equipment in existence that would assure his voice carrying from ringside, and that, even if it should be heard, there were still no radio sets in most parts of the country to receive it.

However, Andy White would not give up. He began to

dig for information. He soon discovered that the General Electric Company had built a special broadcasting set that could be heard all over the land.

With this information, Andy White called together all the important theatre operators in the country and told them that there was a broadcasting set powerful enough to reach the remotest parts of the United States. Did they want to cash in on his idea by installing radio receiving sets in their theatres so that audiences could hear the fight for the heavyweight championship, blow-by-blow, as broadcast direct from ringside?

The response was immediate and enthusiastic. The theatre owners were wild about the idea. They rushed out and bought radio receivers and had them ready for use on the day of the big fight.

With everything seemingly in hand, Andy White now had no difficulty at all in making Tex Rickard agree to permit him to make the broadcast from ringside.

Came the eve of the fight. Everything seemed to be in readiness for the big experiment. Then the blow fell. Andy White learned that the broadcasting set he wished to use belonged to the United States Navy! He would have to get official permission.

In panic, Andy White rushed to the Navy offices to plead his case with the top command. The big brass was adamant against his argument that thousands of people all over the country would be bitterly disappointed if the broadcast were not to take place.

About to give up his cause as hopeless, Andy White finally found one official with enough authority to tell him to use the Navy broadcasting set, that he would take full responsibility for that action.

And so radio history was made, thanks to a Navy man with the courage to take responsibility for an important decision, and to a fellow named Andy White who had the determination to see an idea through. For the first time in radio history, thousands of people throughout the United States heard the coast-to-coast broadcast of an important event.

The name of the man with the idea was, as you now know, Andy White. The official who gave White the all-important permission to use the set was at that time an obscure Assistant Secretary of the Navy. He later became President of the United States. His name was Franklin Delano Roosevelt!

MILLIONS DIED IN EUROPE DURING WORLD WAR II BUT NO man's passing brought more tears to the eyes of sports fans all over the world than that of little Sparrow Robertson, famous boxing columnist of the Paris *Herald*. His memory will be forever green among fight fans.

Sparrow Robertson was born in Edinburgh, Scotland, but came to America as a child and grew up in a tough section of Brooklyn, U.S.A. He always wanted to be a sports hero, and he did manage to make a name for himself as a distance runner. But he always fell short of his ambition. To quench his disappointment, he became a trainer. As such he trained Olympic teams and his job took him through many countries of Europe. Of all the places he went, Sparrow especially enjoyed the gay and easy life of Paris. He determined that some day he would go there to stay.

In World War I, Sparrow went to France as an athletic instructor with the A.E.F. He returned to the States in 1919. America in the spring was beautiful but there was something missing here for Sparrow. He was restless, he missed Paris in the spring, the lights, the laughter, the chestnut trees in bloom.

One day, unable to stand it any longer, Sparrow just

picked himself up, took a boat, and sailed away to that beloved Paree. He had no job, no money, no prospects. It didn't bother Sparrow a bit. He was sure he'd manage somehow. Something would come up. Paris would not let him down.

Sure enough, something did come up for Sparrow Robertson. He landed a job with the Paris *Herald*, as a boxing reporter. As the years passed, Sparrow worked himself up. He became, finally, the sports editor of the *Herald*, and one of the best known figures in Paris. He was to be seen at ringside at every boxing match. Everyone loved the little Sparrow and when sporting celebrities went abroad, it was he who entertained them, took them to Montmartre, the race track, the cafés, even singing to them (if he liked them well enough) his favorite ballads of the gay '90s.

Sparrow's boxing column appeared daily in the Herald and was read all over Europe. He became the staunch ally of Jeff Dickson, most famous boxing promoter in Europe, as well as all the European representatives of American promoters. He was often invited to Hamburg or Berlin to judge or referee important prize fights. But when anyone asked him when he was going back to the States, he would only smile as he answered: "I'll never leave Paris, come what may! Remember, I have a daily column to turn out!"

World War II came. France was crushed. As the German hordes advanced on Paris, the people fled for safety. But Sparrow Robertson refused to leave. Even when the German General Staff moved into his hotel, Sparrow remained where he was. For some strange reason, perhaps out of respect and admiration for the courageous little American, the Germans let him stay in his room, the only civilian in the hotel.

Now Paris was a city of the dead. The gay and brightly lighted metropolis was a ghost of its former self. Nevertheless, Sparrow went on about his business as though nothing unusual had happened. Every morning, Sparrow walked to the offices of the Paris *Herald*, passing the hated Germans without seeing them, and climbed to his office. He sat down at his desk and knocked out his daily boxing column. When he finished he would call out, "Copy Boy! Rush this down to press!"

His voice would echo from the silent walls of that huge newspaper office for the room was completely deserted. All the desks were untenanted. All had long since gone. For the Germans had stopped the publication of the paper as soon as they had reached Paris!

Week after week, month after month, Sparrow Robertson went through his usual ritual. Then, one day, the Germans issued a peremptory order to Sparrow Robertson to stop his ghostly charade. He sought permission to make one last visit to the newspaper office. It was reluctantly granted. Sparrow Robertson, realizing now that his job was finished for good, took the last lingering walk to the Rue Scribe and the offices of the Paris *Herald*. Wearily he climbed the steps to his floor. He sat down at his desk, hesitated a moment, then began to write. It was his last boxing column. Finished, he left the building, walked home. He climbed to his shabby little room of the hotel, lay down, and died. No man passed away with a surer knowledge that he had done his job to the last breath.

BLOOD WILL TELL

Almost at the very moment Jack Johnson knocked out Jim Jeffries to become the first Negro to hold the heavyweight championship of the world, the cry went up for a fighter to regain the title for the white race. Most of the clamor was due to Johnson's wild escapades that had antagonized sport fans all over the world.

The search for a "white hope" ranged far and wide. New heroes loomed upon the sport page, faded rapidly, died. Then a new young fighter, big, handsome, clever, streaked into prominence. With each passing fight, his name became more and more famous, and it was hoped that here at last was the man who could do the job. He knocked out the leading heavies. It seemed a sure bet that Luther McCarthy would some day soon take the coveted crown from the disreputable Jack Johnson.

As a result of Johnson's behavior, boxing was forbidden in almost all parts of the North American continent. It became quite difficult for a rising young heavyweight like Luther McCarthy to get matches.

An opportunity rose for a match with Arthur Pelky, a fair-to-middling heavyweight who was not considered in the same class with McCarthy. And it was set for May 24, 1913 at 1 p.m. in a barn just across the Canadian border.

Only a selected group of spectators was invited to the contest—at one thousand dollars the ticket! Only one man got in free. He was a clergyman who had become friendly with McCarthy and his manager during the training period before the fight. The clergyman's parish was badly in need of funds and he had asked permission to make a short appeal for help from the well-heeled audience.

Shortly before the fight was to start, a new rule was put into effect for the fighters: there was to be absolutely no punching in the clinches. This was done because McCarthy was noted as a punishing infighter and the officials wished to make the fight as even as possible.

It was a dark, dreary, murky day, that 24th of May. The rain came down in torrents as the invited guests slowly arrived in small groups and were whisked into the little barn out of sight of the law. At quarter to one, McCarthy and Pelky climbed into the ring. McCarthy's manager stepped into the center of the ring and asked the announcer to give him a minute's time. The permission was granted. The manager beckoned to the clergyman.

The minister slipped through the ropes and faced the wondering and impatient crowd. He began to speak, haltingly at first as he became aware of the hostility of the crowd. He told them that he himself had once been a boxer but that he was here now only to ask for a little help for his parish which was bitterly in need of funds to go on with its work. Then he hesitated, as he saw that he must somehow make a deeper impression on his listeners.

"Who knows what will happen to any of us?" he cried out passionately. "Here before you stand two wonderful athletes, each in the full flower of youth, each trained to the highest perfection, marvelous physical specimens of American manhood. Who among us dare say that the Great Referee will not count out one or both of these men within the next year, the next month, the next day, nay, the very next hour, if He so will it?" The clergyman paused and a hush fell over the audience. The clergyman waited. Then the buzz of conversation began anew. It seemed that no one had even heard the clergyman's appeal for help. Only in McCarthy's corner, the latter's manager creased his forehead as an odd chill ran down his spine. McCarthy himself became angry as no one responded to the clergyman. He stepped from his corner and shook hands with the bewildered man. "I guess it didn't work, pastor," he said. "But don't let it bother you. We'll think of some other way."

To his manager who stepped up behind him as the clergyman left the ring, McCarthy said, "That's a hell of an audience. They didn't understand a word he said. Now, remember, I want you to give the pastor some dough for me."

McCarthy's manager felt another chill. McCarthy's words added to those of the clergyman seemed too strange, too odd, to be passed over lightly. What did it all mean?

Further speculation stopped abruptly when the first bell rang to call the men to the center of the ring. As McCarthy's manager slipped out between the ropes he called back a last warning to Luther. "Don't forget, kid. Don't hit in the clinches or they'll take it away from you!"

The fight began. Luther McCarthy, sure-footed, clever, supremely confident, charged his opponent from the very start. Pelky back-tracked from the opening bell, warily avoiding the powerful fists of his adversary.

Then it happened, unexpectedly, without warning, the accident that could never take place. McCarthy shifted a little, feinted with his left, drove a sharp right to Pelky's head. Pelky flattened himself against the ropes to which the blow had driven him. As he rebounded from them, McCarthy's manager shouted a sudden warning to his boy in the ring. "He's going to clinch! Look out, now!"

Luther, hearing the familiar voice barking in his ear, chuckled to himself and turned his head to reassure his manager that he had not forgotten the last minute instructions. At the very instant that he turned his head, Pelky started to swing, his clenched fist rising from the very floor towards McCarthy.

Luther's head, turned aside as it was, was in an awkward and unnatural position as it received the full and deadly impact of that desperate blow. There was a sickening crash and Luther staggered, tried to hold his feet, then slowly sank into a crumpled heap on the canvas. In the ensuing silence the referee began to toll the count of ten over the fallen fighter.

Some time in the match the rain had stopped falling outside the barn. The clouds were still overhead when the punch delivered by Pelky dropped McCarthy to the canvas. But as the referee intoned the count over McCarthy a thin ray of sunlight fell on the roof of the barn. It found a tiny crack, came through and into the building, sought out and found its objective. And, as the final number was spoken, Luther McCarthy's face shone in the beam of sunlight and his hair picked up the light like a halo around his head. A moment passed. The beam of light disappeared. The referee straightened up, turned to McCarthy's corner where the fighter's anxious manager was waiting.

One look at his boy's glassy eyes was all the manager needed to take. He shouted for a doctor. Several physicians clambered into the ring. But it was too late. Luther McCarthy was dead. Never again would his name be eagerly spoken when talk of a new "white hope" sprang up. The Great Referee had indeed counted him out as unexpectedly as the humble clergyman had warned only a moment before.

PETE ASERO WAS JUST ANOTHER OF THE THOUSANDS OF kids sweating away in stuffy little gymnasiums, dreaming of the day when their names will blaze in sport headlines.

Pete, a New York boy, was the hero of his neighborhood, having already won an amateur title before turning professional.

There was one thing Pete wanted more than anything else in the world. After every fight in which he took part, Pete would go through the sport pages of the newspapers. When he found a report of his contest, he would shake his head at the two-line item and say, "Never mind, fellows, I'll get my picture in the papers yet. Yes sir, I'll be in there in fighting togs and all, and right on top will be my name in big letters."

Pete went on and on, scrapping in the small clubs for bread and butter money, sometimes getting fifty bucks, sometimes as much as seventy-five for his efforts. He piled up a record of twenty-seven victories and his pals were beginning to talk of a match for the title. However, in spite of his victories, he never got more than the two brief lines on the sports page the following morning.

Then, one day not so long ago, Pete was matched with a fair second-rater and given the promise that a victory would earn him a fight at a bigger club for more money.

On the day of the fight, while Pete was weighing in, he turned to a pal and said, "I think I'm going to make it this time. I feel lucky. Yep, I guess I'll get my picture in the papers this time for sure!"

Pete had all his pals in the galleries rooting for him that night, for the promising young welter was a right guy. And his buddies had a lot to cheer about during the first three rounds. He danced around his opponent and peppered him with sharp stinging lefts and rights. It looked like a breeze for Pete Asero.

Then, in round four, something happened. In mid-ring, boxing easily, Pete suddenly stopped fighting. He turned as white as a sheet and dropped his arms to his sides. Then he tottered a little, his knees gave way and he sank to the canvas.

Pete's seconds jumped quickly into the ring. The referee reached the boy before they did. As they began to plead for a moment's respite to bring him to, the referee straightened up. "The fight's over," he said. "Your boy is dead."

The promising career of Pete Asero was thus ended in tragedy. There is, nevertheless, something to add. In the city's newspapers next morning there was a picture of a fighter in tights near the top of the sports page. The picture bore the name of Pete Asero, poor "lucky" Pete Asero who had to give his life to realize his fondest dream!

THERE ARE MANY REWARDS FOR A MAN WHO WORKS AT THE trade of prize fighting. But the road to ring glory is paved with heartbreak, laved with blood and haunted by the ghosts of fighting men who paid with their lives for the price of ring greatness. Jimmy Doyle discovered that too late.

Jimmy Doyle was a fighter out of Los Angeles, California—a welterweight by trade, who lived for one particular day, a day when he would crawl through the ropes and fight for the welterweight championship of the world. And so, the fame-hungry kid with star-dust in his eyes, went through the boxing mill, winning here and losing there, but always looking forward to that golden day when he would be inside a ring battling for the title.

That day came in the month of June, in the year 1947. At 22, Jimmy Doyle finally had reached his goal. He was facing "Sugar" Ray Robinson, the welterweight champion of the world.

And in that fight, Jimmy Doyle, the kid who always wanted to fight for a ring crown, made boxing history. He was killed—the only time a fighter has been killed as a result of punches in a championship bout.

THERE'S AN OLD SAYING THAT MEN WHO LIVE BY THE SWORD shall perish by the sword. Sam Baroudi was the living and dying proof of it.

Sam Baroudi was a poor kid out of Akron, Ohio. He was a boy hungry for sports fame and some of the gold which he had heard could be found in the ring. So, he became a prize fighter—a heavyweight by trade. And a fantastic dream began whirling in his head that some day he would become a "second Joe Louis." But he wasn't in the ring long before he began to learn that prize fighting is a rough and brutal business, mostly run by shady men who would sell a fighter's life for a buck. And one night in 1947, all the romance of the ring faded for Sam Baroudi. In a bout in North Adams, Massachusetts, Sam Baroudi fought an opponent named Glen Newton Smith, and killed him.

The shock of that tragedy overwhelmed Sam Baroudi. He quit the ring and he tried to forget the horror of that moment which his two fists had created. He tried to escape from the evil men who had lured him into that tragic bout. But for young Sam Baroudi, escape from the ring was not possible. Too soon, he was tempted to return and fight again. However, something had gone out of Sam Baroudi's heart. His return to the trade of prize fighting was a sad mistake. One night in 1948, Sam Baroudi fought a heavyweight named Ezzard Charles. He was killed.

Thus ended a strange story of a prize fighter who killed a man with his fists, only to be killed himself by another fighter's fists.

A TALE OF OLD MEXICO

There was a pretty good fighter some years ago by the name of Harvey Thorpe who might have become a champion in his division except for one thing. Harvey preferred farming to fighting. At just about the time that he was coming to the top of the pack, Harvey bought himself a good-sized farm in Kansas and retired from the ring, as he thought, forever.

He had barely settled down to the peaceful life of a farmer when his former manager, a shrewd character, came running posthaste to visit his fighter with exciting news. "Harvey," he yelled, "it's the break of a lifetime! I can get you a fight with the Mexican champ for a fat purse of $8,000. That's more dough than you ever made before in one fight, Harvey! What do you say, kid, huh? Let's get packed for Mexico and pick up the easy money!"

Harvey, the happy farmer, at first refused to accept the match. The manager would not give up. He continued to dangle the attractive $8,000 before the retired fighter's eyes until at last, and reluctantly, Harvey agreed to fight that last fight in Mexico. One fight, and no more, swore Harvey Thorpe. And on that basis, off they went to Mexico.

It was a hot scorching day that Harvey Thorpe stepped into the ring in Juárez before a mob of wild and shouting Mexican fight fans. As the battle began Harvey Thorpe discovered that the other man in the ring was going to prove an exceedingly tough nut to crack. The two men went at it hammer and tongs. Fifteen savage furious rounds went into the book. Harvey was barely able to stay on his feet, much less lift his tired and leaden arms to throw punches at his opponent. That $8,000 didn't seem to be the easy touch it looked like way back in Kansas that peaceful and quiet morning.

Suddenly a frightened cry went up from hundreds of throats in the arena. There was a burst of rifle fire, screams of anguish. Then, in a great cloud of dust, a large band of shrieking men on horseback swept into the arena. It was a guerilla raid on Juárez, and it was led by none other than that most redoubtable of bandits, Pancho Villa, most feared man in all Mexico.

There was a wild rush to the exits as the spectators learned who their unwelcome visitor was. And Harvey Thorpe who was not only a good fighter but a smart one as well, ducked under the ring, to which shelter he was accompanied by the Mexican champion. A moment later, the bandit boss on his white horse rode up to the edge of the ring. In an imperious voice he ordered the American fighter to crawl out of his hiding place, but pronto!

Villa scowled down at the frightened fighter when he came out blinking in the sun. "Who are you, gringo?" demanded Pancho Villa. "And what are you doing here?"

"I—I'm boxing," stammered Harvey Thorpe. "I came here from my country to fight the Mexican champion. I was promised a purse of eight thousand dollars."

Pancho Villa threw back his head and howled with laughter. "Then let me see you fight, Americano!" he cried. "And I, Pancho Villa, will watch this fight. If you want to be paid, my friend, see to it that you fight well!"

The two fighters, weary and sore after fifteen rounds of hard fighting, climbed back into the ring and began all over again. Five, ten, fifteen rounds they went at it, as furiously as before. Whenever the pace tended to slow down a bit, the bandits at ringside encouraged the boys to harder effort by firing their guns in the general direction of the ring and shrieking for blood or else! After twenty rounds of battling made furious by the sound of bullets whistling around their ears, the fight stopped and the Americano, Harvey Thorpe, was declared the winner.

Pancho Villa rose from his place at ringside and bowed gracefully to the winner in the ring. "Gringo," he said grandly, "you are one good fighter. You deserve all the money they promised you. But," he added with an apologetic shrug, "since I myself am taking all the money in this town I suppose I will have to pay you something. Here, my brave American friend. This bag is for you. Do not open it till I am gone." And, tossing the bag into the ring at Harvey Thorpe's feet, Villa shouted in parting, "You were *magnífico! Adios, amigo!*"

No sooner was the dreaded Pancho Villa out of sight than Harvey Thorpe scooped up the bag at his feet and tore it open to count the gold that the bandit leader had left for him. Would it be more or less than the $8,000 he had been promised?

There was no gold in the bag. Harvey looked at its contents in dismay. Instead of money, there were hundreds of beans, thousands of them, of the plain Mexican garden variety. For thirty-five gruelling rounds of boxing under a broiling hot sun, Harvey Thorpe had been paid off—with a bag of beans.

It was a sad and crestfallen Harvey Thorpe who made his way back to that wonderful farm in Kansas. He was finished with the ring for good. No one would ever get him into the squared circle again. He had learned his lesson.

But wait. The story does not end quite here. Several years after the debacle at Juárez, Pancho Villa was shot down and killed. His funeral was a thing of beauty and pomp. Among the many wreaths and sumptuous floral offerings was a lovely cluster of bean blossoms sent by some unknown admirer from far off Kansas to the dashing and gallant bandit leader of Mexico. With it was a short note. It read:

> "I've got two hundred acres of beans
> planted already. They grow like
> wildfire up here. You too were
> magnificent! *Adios, amigo!*"

KILLING A KILLER

It takes cleverness to be a good fighter but it takes the killer instinct to make a great one. The man without the urge to murder the man in the ring with him may find the road to fame and fortune an elusive one. There is no better proof of this than the story of Hughey Walker.

It was in the fall of the first year of World War I that a handsome kid from Kansas City came into the fistic limelight as a great ring attraction. Back home Hughey Walker had been but a prelim fighter. It was when Walker moved on to Little Rock, Arkansas, that he became hotter than hot. The unknown youngster caused a panic among the Hot Springs gamblers of that era by bowling over favorite after favorite that had been backed by the coin of the sporting fraternity.

A prominent sportsman named Billy McCarney was Hughey Walker's manager at the time. McCarney realized that he had a coming champion in the making in young Walker, so he steered the green young kid away from the tough topnotchers of the ring.

As the gamblers continued losing their money betting against the boy, they set up a great cry for Hughey to meet a big-timer. The mob was eager to see the lad beaten, of course, but they were chiefly concerned with recouping their losses.

The pressure on McCarney finally grew so great that he consented to a match between the boy and the great

Jack Dillon, who happened to be in training at Hot Springs for some big money bouts. Dillon gladly accepted the bout with the green kid, figuring to pick up some extra, easy dough for himself.

Jack Dillon was one of the most feared men in boxing, having earned for himself the nickname of Giant Killer. And the gamblers, happy at the opportunity to regain all they had lost, bet that Jack Dillon would win by a knockout. They gave plenty of odds, too.

The night of the fight saw the arena packed to the rafters. At the opening bell, Jack Dillon, proud, cocky, confident, danced out of his corner to give the fans what they were looking for and show them why he was the greatest middleweight in the world.

The first blow thrown by Dillon almost tore young Hughey Walker's head off. Dillon smiled cruelly and stepped back to watch the green kid fall. The youngster shook off the blow as though it had never been landed. Amazed, Dillon charged in, landing powerful punches with dazzling speed. Hughey took the blows without flinching. In spite of the fearful beating he was taking, he stayed on his feet. In all the first round, Walker landed but one punch on the elusive Jack Dillon.

Hughey went back to his corner, his face a smear of blood. He grinned up at his manager. "Feel fine," he said lightly. "He can't hurt me. I'll lick him."

Manager McCarney looked at his boy in amazement. Was the kid out of his mind? Three minutes of brutal punishment and he was still joking.

The second round was worse than the first. Jack Dillon was trying desperately to knock out his opponent and end the fight. He did not succeed. When blood-covered Hughey Walker returned to his corner, he again whispered to McCarney. "He's slowin' up. He can't hurt me. I'll take him!" And he grinned again.

The third round was a repetition of the butchery of the first two. But the green kid stayed on his feet through it all. And then, in the fourth round, something happened. Dillon threw a whistling right at his opponent and Walker somehow managed to beat him to the punch. Back went Dillon's head under the impact. His mouth flew open and his knees began to buckle. As he began to sink to the canvas he threw out his arms and caught Walker in a desperate clinch. The bell saved Dillon.

Hughey Walker bounced back into his corner and his grin was now wider than ever. "What did I tell you?" he cried out to McCarney. "Told you I'd take him. Here's where I knock him out!"

Manager McCarney must have had a soft streak in his make-up some place. "You've got him, kid," he said. "But don't knock him out. It would break his heart. Look, there'll be other great days for you, you're just a kid on the way up. Let him finish his career without shame. Let him last the distance. After all, the fight is yours."

So Hughey Walker grinned good-naturedly and let sentiment get the best of him. He boxed the groggy Dillon for the rest of the fight and won the decision easily. It was a sad day for the gamblers.

It was, in a way, a sad day for Hughey Walker, too. Failure to score the knockout which was in his grasp spelled the finish of his own title aspirations. Hughey could never again work himself up to great heights in the ring. He became, instead, one of the most durable "catchers" in fistic history. No one could knock him out and he fought them all from middleweight to heavyweight, men like Carl Morris, Bill Brennan, Young Stribling, Harry Greb and Gunboat Smith. Never once was he knocked off his feet by any of them.

However, the spark of genius had fled, the spark kindled in the Dillon fight that might have led to a championship. Had he only gone ahead to knock out the Giant Killer that day, there is no saying how far Hughey Walker would have gone in the ring.

OLDTIMERS WHO FIRST SAW THE HARD-HITTING, SAVAGE MAX Baer step into the ring will tell you that the California Adonis could have been the greatest heavyweight of all had it not been for a single laugh that rang in his ears early in his career. It was that laugh that may have changed a great fighter with a strong killer instinct into the merriest clown that ever pranced through the ropes.

It was in 1930 that Max Baer met a barrel-chested, handsome young Italian named Frankie Campbell. Minutes before the fight was to begin, a trainer told Max in the dressing room that Campbell was saying things about him, calling him a punk and a bum. Baer sprang down from the rubbing table, slapped one glove against the other and yelled, "Okay, let's go! I'll kill this guy!"

In the second round, Frankie Campbell caught Max with a looping right and dumped him to the canvas. Foolishly, Frankie turned to wave at some friends at ringside and laughed in derision. Max, sprawling on the floor, heard the jeering laugh and his rage burst like a storm. He shot across the ring and sent Campbell spinning with a terrific blow behind the ear.

Campbell, spitting blood between rounds, mumbled to his seconds, "I think something snapped in my head." Nevertheless, he went out for the third and fourth rounds to run into a Baer gone berserk. Fighting like a madman to erase the memory of that derisive laugh, Baer punched furiously. In the fifth round he dropped the battered Campbell. The next morning, Frankie died, a horrible, battered wreck of a man.

From that day, Max Baer ceased to be the same vicious

killer of the ring. There was a period of semiobscurity during which Max was on the skids. Then he came back to win other fights, but never again with the full display of savagery that marked him in that fatal bout. His parade through fistiana was thoroughly picturesque. His clowning made all the headlines. Despite his antics, Max fought the best of them, men like Tom Heeney, Max Schmeling, Tommy Loughran, Risko, and Paulino. It was his defeat of Schmeling that earned Max Baer a shot at the title then held by the ponderous Primo Carnera. And that fight was one of the wildest ever seen in the Garden Bowl.

Max, eternally the clown, dominated the fight from start to finish. Although the big Italian outweighed him by nearly seventy pounds, the California Adonis tossed him around the ring like a sack of oats. While winning the title, Max was still able to get off one of his best gags in the ring. Outfighting and outjabbing the big champion, Max sent his opponent to the canvas twelve separate occasions during the contest. Many of the times he was knocked down, Carnera succeeded in grabbing Baer and pulling him with him. Instead of making Max sore, this little trick of the champion's seemed to amuse him more and more each time it happened. At last, when the two men were sprawling on the floor and trying to scramble back to their feet to go on with the fight, Baer turned to Primo lying next to him and roared happily in his ear for all the spectators to hear, "Hey, Preem! Last one up's a sissy!"

MEN WITHOUT TITLES

In a quiet cemetery in far-off Australia, a monument stands before a grave on a little hill. An inscription is carved on that monument. It reads:

"Sleep, Peter, sleep, brave champion. All hushed, we gather around the ring while snow-white flowers, moist-eyed, we fling within the grave. The fight is done. Sleep, Peter, sleep. The hero's rest be thine in Mother Earth's broad breast."

It's an unusual inscription to be carved on a tombstone. The story of the man who lies within that grave is no ordinary one.

Peter Jackson was a modest Negro lad who, at sixteen years of age, was already winning fame as a great all-around athlete in his homeland of Australia. He was best-known as a fine swimmer and diver, and, though few Americans know it, it was he who first introduced the Australian crawl stroke to the United States. Besides, Jackson was noted as record-holder for swimming under water.

To his swimming and diving achievements, Peter added many rowing triumphs, becoming, at one time, Australia's sculling champion.

Peter went to sea at an early age. While aboard ship on one voyage, he was forced into a fist fight with a brutal officer who had almost caused a mutiny because of his cruel treatment of the men. Although greatly outweighed, Jackson licked him severely in a fierce rough-and-tumble battle.

Thus began Peter Jackson's ring career. It was in 1883 in Australia that he first entered the professional ring. He was a magnificent fighting man, both in ability and appearance. Peter stood 6 feet, 1½ inches tall, weighed 192 pounds, and was a picture of grace and rhythm in the ring.

But Peter Jackson could fight. How that man could fight! He was an absolute master of boxing, as fast as a streak, and a terrific hitter. Many have sworn that Peter Jackson was the greatest boxer ever to step into the ring.

Whether he was or not is hard to prove. The fact is, however, that Jackson never seemed to extend himself in his fights. It seemed that he was always under wraps, fighting only hard enough to win or stay even with his adversary.

In a few short years, Peter Jackson had climbed to the top as champion of England and Australia. By 1889, Jackson had licked everyone he could meet in those countries and was ready to seek further for someone to fight.

In Europe, no man would enter the ring with him. He was too dangerous to fight.

Peter Jackson went on to America. By this time, he had determined to get a crack at the world's heavyweight title. He took a few tune-up fights, beating his opponents with consummate ease. It was the worst thing he could have done. The world's champion was John L. Sullivan, whose boast in bars from coast to coast was that he could lick any man in the world. But when Peter Jackson raised his gentle voice in acceptance of the challenge, John L. turned a deaf ear. It might have been better for boxing if Sullivan had given no excuse at all than the one offered. For John L. Sullivan drew the color line. He would not fight a Negro in the ring.

Peter Jackson repeated his challenge again and again.

The word got around that John L. actually feared to meet him. Finally, one leading heavyweight agreed to a match with Jackson. This was a young ex-bank clerk named James J. Corbett. The battle that followed is a memorable one in fistic history. Fought on May 21, 1891, the bout lasted 61 grim bloody rounds. Corbett, a clever and dangerous fighter, was no more than a match for Peter Jackson. It was generally assumed that Jackson, aware of the fact that he would never get another fight in the United States if he won too quickly, "carried" Corbett by stalling off his attack for round after round. In any case, the exhibition given by Jackson fooled nobody. Jackson's superlative ability in the ring was quite obvious. After the Corbett match not only Sullivan but every other American fighter of consequence ducked under the color line as an excuse not to meet this great Negro fighter.

Peter got only three matches during the year following the Corbett draw. For the next six years he was cruelly ignored altogether. Certain that he was the best heavyweight fighter in the world, Jackson ate his heart out as he waited for someone to meet his challenge. All that time he was denied the opportunity to make a living at his chosen profession. He was too good—and black.

From being a happy, carefree man, Peter Jackson turned into a bitter, lonely one, brooding over the injustice of his position. Not once did he complain, not once did he make a whimper. He grew ring-rusty, of course, and lived in poverty.

Finally, when Jackson was 37 years old and a wreck of his once great self due to idleness, grief, hunger and despair, he was matched to fight the young, strong James J. Jeffries. For two rounds, Peter flashed his old-time form, holding off the ponderous boilermaker with ease. In the third round, Peter Jackson's world collapsed around him. Jeffries knocked him out. It was the end of the road for the once-great fighter. Jackson fought only one more time before sailing back to Australia.

At the early age of 40, the broken-hearted man who had once been Peter Jackson passed away prematurely, a victim of tuberculosis.

Upon his death, remorse gripped a world of sport fans who had ignored him during his lifetime. From admiring legions came a flood of money for the purchase of a tombstone to be placed at the head of the dead warrior's grave. What did that silent near-champion think in his cold and final resting place? They say he murmured as he lay dying, "They should have given me a chance to fight . . . they should have given me a chance . . ." It is fitting to end the tale by quoting the words spoken by a great heavyweight champion when he came to the end of his road. "The greatest ring warrior that ever lived," said Gentleman Jim Corbett, "was Peter Jackson."

MANY AN OLDTIMER WILL TELL YOU THAT JACK JOHNSON, first Negro heavyweight champion of the world, was the cleverest of the champions. "Li'l Artha," as he was known, beat them all in his day. All, that is, except one, a stocky little man feared throughout fistiana as the famed "Boston Tar Baby," Sam Langford. Langford, also a Negro, roamed the highways and byways, meeting and beating the best men he could lure into the ring with him. But he never could get Johnson to agree to a title match. Some people called Sam the uncrowned heavyweight champion of the world. Proud little Langford wanted no empty honors. He yearned, instead, for a chance to win the crown in honest combat. He chased the champion up and down the land, hurling challenge after challenge, but to no avail. "Li'l Artha" wanted no part of him, simply refusing to make the match. As a matter of fact, champion Jack Johnson never even met Sam Langford face to face—until one night in a Boston tavern frequented by the sporting gentry.

Champion Jack Johnson was standing at the bar surrounded by his admirers when Sam Langford came in and spotted him. The "Boston Tar Baby" waddled over to the bar. "Hello, Johnson," he drawled. "I've been wanting to see you for a long, long time. I've got something I'd like to ask you."

The excited and happy chatter of that packed saloon suddenly died away into silence. The men at the bar slowly edged away leaving Johnson and Langford together.

"I've been chasing you a long time," went on Langford. "You've been ducking me right along. When are you going to fight me?"

Jack Johnson, who feared no one, looked down at the little man. "I'm not bothering to fight you, Sam," he said. "There ain't nothing in it for me."

With that, Johnson picked up his stick and gloves and started for the door. Bulky little Sam Langford planted himself directly in the big man's path. "I'm not looking for any money out of this," he said quietly. "I jus' know I can lick you, that's all, and I want everybody in this room to hear me tell you so to your face. I've got a thousand dollars in my pocket. I'm going to leave it right here on the bar. You and I will go down to the cellar and have it out, once and for all. Whoever comes up first takes the money. In fact, you can have the thousand even if I beat you. You got to give me a crack at your title!"

Jack Johnson grinned his golden smile and began to pull on his gloves. "Look, Sam," he said, "I got a new suit on and a new hat and silk shirt. I don't aim to mess them up. Besides, I don't need a thousand dollars. Out of my way, man, I'm leaving."

With that flip remark, Jack Johnson made for the door. Sam Langford turned to watch him leave. "Johnson!" he shouted after the departing champion of the world. "You're scared of me, that's what! I want everybody to hear that. You're scared to fight me!"

Publicly humiliated as he was that night, Jack Johnson never did meet little Sam Langford in the ring for the title. To this day, many still argue that the "Boston Tar Baby" would have become heavyweight champion of the world if given the chance. Unfortunately for him, the closest he ever came to the title was in a Boston tavern trying to start a fight that never was fought.

How well the citizens of Abilene remembered Eisenhower's prowess with his fists is proved by a story about the great general's youth. Although Ike won some measure of athletic fame at West Point, hard luck dogged him at every turn. He went out for football, broke his leg. The same injury prevented him from showing what a great baseball player he was. However, hard luck or no, the Abilene youngster showed that he could use his fists. He could box. More than that, his punch had the kick of a mule.

One summer, the young cadet came back to Abilene to spend his vacation with his family. He was looking forward to a quiet summer of rest and relaxation. It happened, however, that at the same time another man was stopping in the town of Abilene, Kansas. He was a professional prize fighter, a big, husky chap who had won a number of bouts through the West.

The prize fighter was a loud-mouthed boaster who delighted in strutting around the town with the challenge that he could lick anyone in the state of Kansas. He became so obnoxious that one day the publisher of the home town paper decided to shut the fellow up once and for all. He declared, in public print, that the visiting prize fighter was nothing more than a bag of wind, and that there lived a college youngster in Abilene who had never been inside a prize ring but who could lick him in a fight at any distance.

The claim infuriated the visiting pug. His boasts became more abusive. He dared the college kid to accept a fight!

To uphold the reputation of the town and the local publisher, young Ike accepted the challenge.

The fight stirred Abilene as no event had ever done before. For days before the match took place, the natives talked about nothing else. Many bets were made on the home town boy.

The faith of the local populace in young Ike proved amply justified. The Abilene youngster made short work of the blabber-mouthed professional, knocking him out in two rounds.

After the fight many offers poured into young Eisenhower's home. Money was dangled temptingly before him to follow the career of a professional prize fighter. Young Ike turned them down firmly. He went back to school to learn the kind of fighting that he really cared for. And, though he might have reached the pinnacle of success in the prize ring, there is no American who will say that General Dwight D. Eisenhower chose wrongly.

FRIENDSHIP IS WHERE YOU FIND IT

The year 1914 is noteworthy in boxing for several reasons. In that year Joe Louis was born. And in that year the ring world buzzed with talk about Ruby Bob Fitzsimmons who was hanging up his gloves for good at the advanced age of 52. An old heavyweight champion was passing into retirement as a champion of the future was making his appearance on the scene.

There are plenty of people still around who remember Ruby Bob and his famous solar plexus punch. Fitz was an odd-looking figure in the ring. Weighing barely 165 pounds, his spindly legs carried a body with shoulders that spread like those of a blacksmith. You could hardly call him more than a middleweight if you looked at that thin girlish waist but when you saw those long powerful freckled arms you knew why Ruby Bob was the most feared man in the ring.

Fitzsimmons is mainly noted as a holder of three titles in the ring, the middleweight, light-heavyweight and heavyweight. He ruled the roost with iron fists until he was 37. When he was crowding 40, Jim Jeffries loomed up to challenge the champion for his crown. Outweighing Fitz by 55 pounds and 13 years younger, Jeffries proved more than Fitz could handle. The champion broke his hands in the early milling. Helpless, he asked big Jeffries to knock him out. The boilermaker obliged.

Although shorn of his crown, Ruby Bob continued fight-

ing for another 15 years! Then, after more than 35 years
of ring warfare, Fitzsimmons hung up his gloves. It seems
that the great one-time champion must have sensed that
another champion worthy to hold the heavyweight crown
had just then been born.

There is another facet to the career of Bob Fitzsimmons
that is less well-known but no less interesting. Fitz was
crazy about animal pets. Had you been able to wander
into his home while the champion was asleep, you would
have seen an almost unbelievable sight. Surrounding him
in bed would be a varied array of dogs. Curled up comfortably at the champion's toes was his favorite pet, a half-
grown lion.

The half-grown lion was named Nero. Fitz wouldn't
train for a fight unless Nero was standing nearby. Fitz's
handlers were scared to death of the animal, often running away from camp and leaving the champion to carry
on with his training alone. The lion went wherever Fitz
did. Then one day Nero in a playful mood reached out to
cuff an innocent-looking wire. The wire happened to be
a live one, and that was the end of Nero.

After Nero's death, Fitz was inconsolable. There were
still any number of cats, dogs, and snakes in his entourage
but the loss of Nero had left a big gap in the champion's
life. So off he went on a visit to the Bostock Animal Circus. He stopped before a cage which contained four young
lions. Ruby Bob's eyes widened in appreciation.

"My," he murmured, "I'd sure like to have one of those
babies!"

The owner who was standing at his elbow overheard the
remark. "Tell you what, Bob," he said with a grin. "You
can have one. Just you go in and help yourself!"

"Swell!" shouted the champion. "Open the cage!"

"Wait a minute!" said the alarmed circus owner. "Those

lions just chased their trainer out of there. They almost killed him!"

Fitz grinned and opened the door of the cage. He stepped inside boldly and began to talk to the beasts in soothing tones as a mother might to a child. The lions growled and looked threatening but Fitz held his ground firmly. Then, when the animals had calmed down a little, Bob picked up one of the 100-pound jungle terrors and walked out of the cage with his prize. The circus owner looked on flabbergasted.

Fitz took the lion home and named him Senator. Never were there better friends than the tall prize fighter and that handsome young lion. Senator was like a kitten when Fitz was around, rubbing against him and whining and purring with joy at sight of his beloved master.

But the lion grew older and, in the way of beasts, became surly and unmanageable. One day, Senator really reverted to type and attacked Ruby Bob's favorite horse. Hearing the commotion outside Fitz leaped out to see Senator on the horse's back preparing to sink his fangs into the helpless creature. Fitz lunged forward and clouted Senator a terrific wallop on the nose. The blow knocked the lion cold!

As soon as Fitz realized what he had done he broke into tears. "I've killed my lion! I've killed Senator," he howled.

Mrs. Fitz dashed out of the house and took in the scene at a glance. "Heave a bucket of water on him, Bob," she said. "You know how to bring them back after a knockout."

Fitz dumped pail after pail of cold water over the unconscious lion's head until at last the unhappy king of the jungle came to his senses. Ruby Bob had scored one of the longest knockouts on or off the record in his history of fist-swinging.

The big blow also brought to a close a beautiful friendship between man and beast. The horse was patched up, but for the safety of all, Senator, Ruby Bob's favorite pet, was banished to the nearest zoo. It was with tear-filled eyes that the great champion saw his dearest and closest pal carried off. No other pet ever took the place of that shaggy beast in the heart of Ruby Bob Fitzsimmons.

JACKIE FIELDS AND JOE SALLAS WERE A COUPLE OF PALS IN Los Angeles, great pals. What they had, they owned in common, be it money or an ice cream soda. Joe was a little the older of the two and, being handy with his fists, began to teach his buddy the fine art of boxing. The two boys began to haunt the gyms and spar around together. It was always Joe, the older lad, who won.

1924 was an Olympic year and the two boys were eager for a chance at the amateur championship of the world. They entered the competition for the Olympic boxing team, each hoping that the other would be selected too, so that they could eventually go to Paris together.

They survived preliminary eliminations on the West Coast and came on to Boston where the finals were to be held. Joe, as was to be expected, made the team easily by winning the A.A.U. featherweight title. But Jackie, also a featherweight, got whipped in an early bout and was to be left behind when the Olympic squad went to Europe.

Joe Sallas was heartbroken that his pal, Jackie Fields, had not made the team. He begged the officials to give the boy a chance to go along. Another boxing coach added his plea to that of Joe Sallas. Finally the Olympic officials relented and permitted Jackie Fields to make the trip as an alternate. The two buddies were beside themselves with joy. They were not going to be separated after all.

There were many contestants in Paris for the Olympic title in the featherweight division. Jos Sallas, the hot favorite, and his pal Jackie Fields, mowed their way through the opposition until, miracle of miracles, only they two were left at the end to fight it out for the coveted crown.

It was not the first time the boys had met in the ring. On every previous occasion Joe Sallas, the older and more experienced, had won easily. On this night, with the world's amateur championship at stake, the Paris sports arena was jammed to the rafters. The two kids brought the house down with the scrap they put on.

But the fight did not follow the book. After a fierce battle, it was Jackie Fields who was pronounced the victor, not Joe Sallas.

With tears in his eyes, Jackie Fields waited in the center of the ring for his best friend to come over and congratulate him. Everyone expected that Joe would throw his arms around the victor's shoulders and thus confirm the friendship that was between them. But nothing of the sort happened. Joe Sallas, too, was weeping as the contest ended. From that day on, Joe never spoke to his old friend again. And even though a few years later Jackie Fields turned professional and eventually won the welterweight championship of the world, no word ever passed between him and his one-time buddy, Joe Sallas.

THERE WAS A 14-YEAR-OLD KID IN SCHOOL IN BANGOR, Maine, long ago who was pretty handy with his fists. Young as he was the big boys learned to steer clear of him. In a short time, the kid held the reputation of being the best fighter in school.

It happened one day that the boy was kept in after hours for some infraction of the rules. He didn't like it, but he was perfectly willing to accept the punishment. His teacher, a stern wiry Scot, felt that mere detention wasn't enough and decided to whip him as well.

When the teacher came at him with the switch upraised, the schoolboy rebelled. He ducked the first blow and then with a deft thrust yanked the switch from the man's grasp.

With a howl of rage the teacher doubled his fists and charged the schoolboy. A rousing brawl followed which did not last long. Several well-directed blows laid the big Scot flat on his back.

When the teacher came to his senses, he stared wonderingly at the schoolboy, then grinned through cracked lips. "Ye fought fair, laddie," he said. "I won't be taking that away from ye. I'm thinkin' ye have the makings of a good fighter."

The teacher and the schoolboy clasped hands, cementing a friendship that was to last for the rest of their lives. The boy, constantly encouraged by the teacher he had licked, went on to become a professional prize fighter. What is more, he became one of the most remarkable fighters the ring has produced. As one of the great lightweight champions, he ruled the division for eleven years, the longest reign of any lightweight champion in history!

Finally, he retired as undefeated lightweight champion of the world, having met and defeated every challenger that could be found. The schoolboy who beat up his teacher will ever be remembered as the immortal Jack McAuliffe, the Napoleon of the prize ring.

WHEN THE GREAT CHAMPION, JOHN L. SULLIVAN, WAS A BOY, one of his dearest friends was another Irish kid named McDonald. The two played and adventured together in the poorer section of Boston until they grew up to young manhood. Then both decided to become fighters. At the start of their respective careers they swore an oath never to meet each other, in the ring, no matter what happened.

Sullivan, as everyone knows, went on to the heavyweight championship of the world but McDonald never got anywhere in his chosen career. Nevertheless, he remained a firm and loyal friend to the great John L., even to the extent of going into action with his fists to protect Sullivan's name and reputation.

As the years passed, John L. became more and more arrogant while finding it harder and harder to stay away from the bright lights and the companions who followed him wherever he went. McDonald became very unhappy as he watched the once mighty Sullivan waste his robust health and marvellous physical condition.

Then Sullivan was matched to meet the dancing dude known as Jim Corbett. From the beginning, John L. belittled his opponent-to-be and boasted all over town about what he would do to the impudent bank clerk who dared to think he could beat him.

It was with difficulty that McDonald prevailed on Sullivan to go into training. Sullivan finally did so, but a few days before the fight, he went on a binge. His friend sought him frantically all over town. The night before the fight, he found John L. standing at the bar of a New Orleans saloon and making his usual boast that he could lick any so-and-so in the house. McDonald pleaded with his friend to leave the saloon and go home to bed. Sullivan, somewhat the worse for wear, refused point blank. The voices of the two friends rose higher and higher, their tempers hotter and hotter. Finally, McDonald blew his top completely.

"You're drunk!" he shouted. "You're out of condition for your fight tomorrow. What's more, I could lick the stuffings out of you myself right now!"

Angrily, Sullivan made a mighty swipe at his friend and McDonald swung back. The blow smashed Sullivan in the face and knocked him down. Roaring with rage, Sullivan leaped to his feet and went for his pal. There followed, in that New Orleans saloon, one of the fiercest battles ever seen. After several minutes of bitter fighting, McDonald brought up a terrific punch that exploded full force in Sullivan's face. Down went the champion for keeps. McDonald looked sadly down on his fallen friend, then turned and walked out without another word. He never again saw Sullivan.

The next day, John L. Sullivan met Jim Corbett in the ring and was toppled from his heavyweight throne. And, while the record books give that date—September 7, 1892 —as the downfall of the mighty John L., there are a number of oldtimers who will tell you that Sullivan really lost his title one night before, not in the ring but in a New Orleans saloon, at the hands of his own most loyal and faithful friend.

EVERY VISITING DAY AT A WELL-KNOWN STATE INSTITUTION for the insane, a dapper little man in his fifties, hale and hearty though he bears the scars of ring warfare, comes to see one of the inmates. He brings the sick man little gifts of cigarettes and candy and as he hands him the package, always asks, "How are you, kid?" There is never any reply. The inmate looks blankly at his visitor, then turns his head away. He no longer recognizes anyone.

Still, there was a time when these two little men were the principals in one of the most controversial incidents that has ever taken place in the ring. It occurred on July 4, 1912.

Ad Wolgast was lightweight champion of the world. His most persistent and bitterest rival for the crown was a fierce little Mexican pepper pot named Joe Rivers, one of the hardest-hitting lightweights of all time.

The match between the two men was a natural, and at last it was made. Once in the ring they slammed into each other with no mercy asked or given. For twelve brutal, hectic rounds, Wolgast and Rivers stood toe to toe, slugging away for all they were worth. Stubbornly, neither fighter gave ground. Neither went down.

When the bell rang opening the thirteenth round, both fighters lunged at each other desperately, determined to bring the match to an end by a knockout. Joe Rivers lashed out with a terrific right that landed in Wolgast's face with a sickening thud. Wolgast staggered under the impact but he did not go down. As the furious Mexican, scenting the kill, unleashed another haymaker, Wolgast leaped in and whipped a murderous left hook to Rivers' body. Both blows landed simultaneously. Wolgast, clipped on the jaw, began slowly to sink. Before he reached the canvas, the Mexican caved in and dropped to the floor in fearful agony.

It was a clean double knockout, as rare and unusual a sight as ever was seen in the prize ring. Jack Welch, the referee, was momentarily confused. Then, suddenly coming to his senses, he stepped forward, grabbed the prostrate Wolgast under the arms and hauled him to his feet. Holding the semi-conscious champion as nearly upright as possible, Welch began to count out the challenger who still stretched out.

The Mexican managed to get to his feet just as the referee counted ten. The crowd around the ring was in an uproar. Fist fights broke out in a hundred places. It was claimed that the bell had rung before the count had been completed. In the hubbub, Welch, the referee, made for the safety of his hotel, surrounded by a cordon of police.

From the safety of his hotel, Welch announced that his decision stood: Wolgast was the winner by a knockout. The screaming and howling that went up from Rivers' backers could be heard for miles. Arguments, pro and con, went on for weeks. To this very day, anyone can start a row about the Wolgast-Rivers fight. No two people who saw it could agree on what had happened.

Many years have passed since that memorable fight in 1912. Time has taken its toll. The two principals in that hotly-contested double knockout have greatly altered. One of them is still among us, a hale and hearty veteran of many battles. The other abandoned by most of his old friends, has been locked away from society, a battered hulk with a shattered mind.

Which is the hale and which the sick? It is Ad Wolgast, once loudly cheered as the lightweight champion of the world, who is now hopelessly insane and confined in a state institution. And, curiously enough, it is Joe Rivers, the former champion's rival in that ever-disputed double knockout, who remains to this day the most faithful visitor that pathetic Ad Wolgast has!

ONE NIGHT, IN INDIANAPOLIS, A POWERFUL HEAVYWEIGHT fighter named Chuck Wiggins met a big lumbering giant named Joe Packo in a bout. The fight was one of the roughest that anyone present had ever seen. Wiggins, never known as a dancing dude with fine manners in the ring, smacked poor Joe with everything but the water pail. By the time the last bell had sounded, Joe Packo had been introduced to more elbows, thumbs and knees than he had ever thought existed.

After the fight was over, Joe agreed to fight another bout with the tough Mr. Wiggins, the rematch to be held in Grand Rapids. On the afternoon of that encounter, the two men met in the hotel's billiard room. With great amiability, Wiggins invited his opponent to join him in a game of pool. By the time the game ended, the two fighters were fast friends. Wiggins, particularly, was gracious to a fault, expressing concern for Joe's health and wishing him the best of luck in the fight.

"Listen, Chuck," said Packo as they were about to part. "I don't mind you fighting as hard as you can. I expect that in the ring. But how about cutting out the rough stuff tonight? And the fouling, too, huh?"

Wiggins threw his big arm around his pal's shoulders. "Sure, Joe," he said. "You got nothing to worry about. I like you, Joe. It's only that I lost my noodle in our other fight. So don't worry, pal. Just remember, I like you!"

That night Joe Packo and Chuck Wiggins crawled through the ropes for their tête-à-tête. For the first two rounds it was just a nice pleasant scrap. In the third round, Chuck Wiggins got a little playful. He began to use his thumbs, elbows and knees. At first, Joe Packo, sweet simple soul that he was, took it all in good humor. Then, in self-preservation, he began to respond in kind. The fight got so wild and rough that the referee jumped out of the ring in the fourth round, and stayed out. The absence of this official didn't stop the two fighters. They went at it with redoubled gusto. Joe was taking a terrific lacing from his pal, Chuck Wiggins, when, in the sixth round, he was punched to the floor and his head landed on the canvas outside the ropes.

Right where he fell, at ringside, sat Mrs. Chuck Wiggins, enjoying her husband's antics with great glee. When she saw the inviting target presented by the top of the fallen warrior's head, Mrs. Wiggins leaned down, removed one of her high-heeled shoes, and began to belt poor Joe's noggin in a steady tattoo. At each clout, Mrs. Wiggins let out a joyous scream. "Murder 'im, Chuck! Kill the bum!"

When the fight came to a merciful end, Joe Packo looked as though he had been dragged through a buzzsaw. His head was badly cut by Mrs. Wiggins' energetic application of shoe leather, his face was swollen from Chuck's blows, his eyes were tightly closed by that worthy's thumbs.

He was a sorry mess as he sat, alone and mournful, in his hotel room that night. Suddenly there was a cheerful knock on the door. Then the door burst open. In came Chuck Wiggins, dragging a case of beer after him.

"Here's a little present for you, Joe, old pal," said Chuck. "I've come to invite you to my party. My wife and I are celebrating."

Joe Packo raised his swollen face and almost sightless eyes to the happily smiling Chuck Wiggins. "What the blazes do you want me at your party for?" he mumbled. "Especially after that fight?"

Chuck's mouth fell open in surprise. "Gee, Joe," he said in hurt tones. "Don't talk like that. You're my pal, Joe. You know I like you!"

Joe turned his head aside and did not answer. Chuck looked down at him for a minute, and then his face brightened. "Not only that," he added, "my wife likes you too! Honest, Joe, she's crazy about you! Now will you come to my party?"

A FEUD FOR YOUR TASTE

In the long history of ring warfare there have been many feuds among fighters. Most of them were understandable, but not all. Take for example, the bitter feud that started simply because of a high hat. It led to one of the bloodiest battles in ring history.

Around the turn of the century two great lightweights loomed large among the ring men of the time. One was Jimmy Britt, the other Battling Nelson. The fighters were as unlike as they could be. Britt was young, handsome, intelligent, a smooth dandy who not only acted like a perfect gentleman but looked the part in his Prince Albert coat and high hat. On the other hand, Battling Nelson, the Durable Dane, was a hardboiled, tough little man with a weazened face and a tangled mop of wiry hair that defied the discipline of a comb and brush. Nelson's idea of fashion consisted of turtle-neck sweater and a cap.

However, both Nelson and Britt were great lightweights. Britt was a boxing master, Nelson a rugged slugger. Both had their eyes on the lightweight crown.

One day, Battling Nelson, attired in his tasteful ensemble of sweater and cap caught a glimpse of Jimmy Britt in his smart Prince Albert and shiny high hat. The idea of a prize fighter wearing a hat like that positively infuriated the little tough guy. He determined on the spot to destroy Jimmy Britt together with his fancy clothes, slick manners, and, above all, his high hat.

It was inevitable that these two fighters meet in the ring. They came to face each other in a crowded arena under the hot blue sun of a California sky. As Nelson glared across the ring at calm Jimmy Britt, he could still see the high hat in his mind's eye.

When they met in the middle of the ring, Jimmy Britt looked into Battling Nelson's face and what he saw there sent a cold chill down his back. Nelson's eyes were those of a dead man, expressionless, terrifying. Jimmy Britt shook off the feeling with difficulty. He had never been afraid of any man in the ring, and he would not let himself be frightened now.

As the bout began, Britt drew murmurs of appreciation from the crowd for his superb boxing. He landed six times as often as the grim little Nelson, and his blows were hard and sharp. The Durable Dane shook them off and kept ploughing in.

Soon, Nelson's expressionless face was a mass of crimson jelly. With every blow landed by the clever Britt, Nelson shook himself, and muttered in Britt's ear, "I'll lick you. You and your high hat."

For fourteen rounds, Jimmy Britt cut Battling Nelson to ribbons and the Dane kept coming back for more. Britt, at the end of his patience, and somewhat battered and groggy himself from the unending charge of his opponent, stopped boxing and stood toe to toe, slugging it out with Nelson. He began to realize that his adversary was determined to destroy him, and that a beating was not enough for the Durable Dane to take from the ring in victory. The constant snarl of Battling Nelson, "I'll lick you, you with your high hat!" made Britt realize at last that Nelson was fighting him with hate in his heart.

At the start of the eighteenth round, Battling Nelson tore into Jimmy Britt, showering him with club-like rights and lefts. The handsome, superb boxing master, Jimmy

Britt, went down. A hush fell over the arena. The idol of the crowd had crumbled before the fists of the scrubby tough little guy from the Middle West.

Britt's eyes were glazed as he rolled over and tried to pick himself up from the canvas. Nelson, a mass of bruises and beaten to a pulp himself, leaned over the fallen warrior, snarling with hate.

Britt tried desperately to pull himself to his feet to go on with the battle. As Nelson growled with animal satisfaction, Britt's head sank once more to the canvas and the referee counted him out.

Then came the roar of the crowd for the conqueror. Battling Nelson was hailed as a king, swept up on the shoulders of his new admirers and carried triumphantly from the ring.

From this height, Nelson looked down on Jimmy Britt as the latter was being helped to his corner. "Let him wear his high hat now," snarled the new favorite. "He'll never be the champion!"

Battling Nelson was right. Britt never did become champion. Battling Nelson did, thanks to a feud that started because he could not bear to see another fighter wear a high hat.

MANY YEARS AGO, IT WAS THE CUSTOM FOR PRIZE FIGHTERS to come out of their corners with the first round gong, shake hands, step away, and then and only then, start fighting. But for many years now, prize fighters have shied away from the custom—and it's all because of a handshake in a ring on September 7, 1908, a handshake that resulted in the goriest ring duel of all time.

In 1908, Stanley Ketchel was undisputed possessor of the middleweight crown. In case your memory is a little hazy, let me remind you that Ketchel was just about the greatest middleweight in boxing history, the most savage fighter of them all.

There was another great fighter on the scene while Ketchel was champ. He was Billy Papke. Papke was jealous of Ketchel, and always anxious to meet him for the middleweight title. He challenged the titleholder and his challenge was accepted. The match took place in Los Angeles on September 7, 1908.

As the bell rang for the beginning of that first battle, Stanley Ketchel advanced to the center of the ring and extended both gloves for the customary handshake. Wily Billy Papke, out to win at any cost, had a little scheme in his head which he put into immediate execution. At the exact moment that Ketchel put out his gloves for the handshake, Papke lunged in with his entire body back of the punch, he drove a terrific left hook to Ketchel's jaw and followed up with a thundering right. The first punch alone all but knocked the champion out.

Ketchel never fully recovered from that double cross punch. Though he weathered the storm in the first round, Ketchel took a fearful beating from the fists of Billy Papke. For eleven bloody rounds he fought, though he was completely out on his feet. Finally, he was knocked unconscious in the twelfth round just as the police jumped into the ring to stop the slaughter. Billy Papke became the new champion of the middleweights.

It was many hours after the fight before Stanley Ketchel finally recovered and realized what had happened to him. A murderous anger burned in his heart. He determined to make Papke pay for the trick he had played on him. And he kept his plan of revenge to himself.

Shortly after the fight, Ketchel went to San Francisco and hunted up an intimate friend. This friend was then sent to see the most important promoter for the purpose of arranging a return match between the dethroned cham-

pion and his successor. A secret deal was made whereby
the promoter was to offer Papke a big purse and Ketchel
was to guarantee whatever loss the promoter might suffer
if the house were not a sellout.

Thus the stage for revenge was partly set. There was
more to be done to make the bait even more tempting.
Ketchel began to live high, wide and handsome and care
was taken that reports of Ketchel's riotous living reached
Papke, who was told that Ketchel was badly out of condition.

The combination of the reports and the fat purse proved
too much for Papke to resist. He agreed to a return bout.
The battle was held in San Francisco on November 26,
1908. The house was jammed. And there was no handshak-
ing that night.

There may have been bloodier fights in ring history,
but there never was a more savage one than the Ketchel-
Papke return. All the savagery was on Ketchel's part. He
handed Papke the worst licking ever dished out to a prize
fighter.

Ketchel tore into Billy Papke like a madman. There
was murder in his heart to go with the dynamite in his
gloves. Ketchel refused to knock out Billy Papke. As soon
as the champion seemed about to go down, Ketchel would
let up in order to give him a breathing spell, only to start
all over again. The fans pleaded with him to knock Papke
out, but Ketchel refused to finish his man. Finally, in the
eleventh round, the police stopped the fight and the slaughter.

When the battered and bleeding Billy Papke was brought
home after the fight, his own sister refused to admit him
because she failed to recognize him. Stanley Ketchel, only
middleweight to regain the crown after losing it until
Tony Zale turned the trick on Rocky Graziano in 1948,

had earned himself a rich revenge for a handshake that never took place.

Billy Papke never amounted to much after that second fight with Ketchel. Stanley had ruined him for good. And the lives of these two men, linked as they are by this story, are joined in another, and more tragic way. Ketchel died by a bullet from a gun fired at him by a jealous farmhand; Papke took his own life by blowing out his brains.

I GET A KICK OUT OF LISTENING TO THE FIGHT CUSTOMERS argue whether this boy or that one can go ten rounds or fifteen without getting tired. I can't help but remember the oldtimers who thought nothing of laying it on the line for thirty, forty, fifty, even seventy-five rounds to a decision. And what about that famous struggle between Andy Bowen and Jack Burke?

More than half a century ago, Bowen and Burke were a couple of good lightweights who plied their trade down South. Bowen was from Louisiana, Burke from Texas. Each considered himself the best lightweight ever to don leather, and the insults flew back and forth as the two men fought their way up and down the land of Dixie.

The rivalry was bitter before the two boys were finally matched for the lightweight championship of the South. The contest had turned into a grudge affair. It was arranged to be fought at the Olympic Club in New Orleans on April 6, 1893, and a purse of twenty-five-hundred dollars was the prize as well as a thousand-dollar side-bet.

On the night of the fight, New Orleans was at feverpitch. The fight arena was jammed to the rafters. Little did anyone in the packed house realize that he was sitting in on a history-making event.

The battle was bloody. The two men went twenty rounds. They went forty, sixty, eighty. Still there was no decision.

Not a spectator left the arena as the struggle continued. The minutes and hours went by. The night dragged into dawn, the rounds piled up as the sporting men sat in stunned and fascinated silence.

With the first light of day the weary referee stepped between the two boys and called a halt to the long contest. One hundred and ten rounds had been fought, lasting seven hours and nineteen minutes! The bout between Andy Bowen and Jack Burke remains to this day the longest continuous prize fight in history.

And who was awarded the decision in that epic struggle between two lightweights for the championship of the South? No one! The grudge fight that had gone one hundred and ten rounds was stopped by the referee who declared it—"No contest!"

DON'T THROW ROCKS AT FIGHTERS

The man in the limelight makes a tempting target for those of us who are ever ready to toss rocks at him for some not-too-well-understood shortcoming. It isn't always true, though, that our unkind judgments are deserved. Take, for example, Les Darcy, the fellow who was branded by the public in the first World War.

Les Darcy was a prize fighter, an Australian who, some thirty years ago, was one of the outstanding middleweights of the world. Back in his native land, Darcy whipped all the good ones, fellows like Chip, McGoorty, Crouse, and Murray. His skill soon excited the imagination of the American sports public. Before long, there was a great clamor to see Les Darcy in action in an American ring.

Those were war days, however. Just the same, Les Darcy took a job as a deck hand on a tank steamer and slipped out of Australia, bound for the United States. As soon as he arrived on these shores, he began to angle for fights.

At about the same time, there was another ringman in Europe named Georges Carpentier. Gorgeous Georges was an aviator, a gay, handsome fistic hero who had licked a lot of good men himself, fellows like Willie Lewis, Jeff Smith, and others, as well as holding Billy Papke and Frank Klaus even in bruising fights. With Les Darcy in the country looking for action, the wily Tex Rickard, scenting a possible million-dollar attraction, immediately went to work on what seemed a natural.

Once the two were matched, the publicity mills began to grind overtime. The proposed fight steamed up so much comment and ballyhoo, involved such fantastic claims, and so dazzled the public with tales of the vast sums the fighters were to receive, that soon questions began to be asked. How come Les Darcy was to receive so much money with his country fighting for its life in a great war? And why wasn't the Aussie in uniform anyhow? It wasn't long before that short ugly word of World War I began to be heard. The whisper started softly, rose in volume. "Slacker! Slacker! Les Darcy is a slacker!"

Soon the cry was being shouted from the rooftops. Hate and hysteria poured like a flood from the lips of thousands of sports followers. Even thoughtful and reasonable people forgot themselves momentarily. No one stopped to ask why. The Australian was branded from coast to coast with the most insulting name given during war time. Slacker!

Les Darcy became enmeshed in the whirlpool. Everywhere he went to fight, the local patriots attacked him. In several states, the legislatures passed laws preventing Les Darcy from plying his trade within their boundaries. Sports reporters, editorial and feature writers hungry for copy, pounded away on their typewriters, grinding out all sorts of fantastic nonsense about Les Darcy. Every pen was dipped in acid.

For Les Darcy, the whole business was like a dark cloud that had suddenly burst over him, drenching him with choking poison. No matter how hard he tried to answer the charges levelled against him, he could find no one willing to listen.

The abuse and ridicule, the hate and persecution, all served to help crush Darcy. His world was shattered.

He became at last a brooding, silent, bitter and beaten man. Nowhere in the United States could he get a fight.

Then, one night, in Memphis, Tennessee, he came down with a slight cold. It wasn't a serious illness at all, but Les Darcy had neither the heart nor the will to fight it. The cold quickly developed into pneumonia. The doctors tried their utmost to save his life, but Les Darcy just lay on his hospital bed, staring vacantly into space. He seemed to be glad he was dying.

Despite the care he was given, Les Darcy passed away. The doctors gave the cause of death as pneumonia, but there were many who were sure that Les Darcy died of a broken heart.

And there is an epilogue to the story, of course, a cruel and ironic one. Soon after Les Darcy's tragic death, it was revealed that he had volunteered not once but three times for military service. And three times the British Army had rejected Darcy as unfit on the grounds that his vision was too impaired. Far from being a slacker, Les Darcy was a victim of harsh and hasty criticism because he stood so far above the common man and made so tempting a target.

BACK IN 1917, THE GREAT LITTLE PETE HERMAN WAS BANtamweight champion of the world. No one was faster than he, no man could hit as hard. In his day, he licked the best in his class and even featherweights and lightweights.

Then the first World War came. Prize fighters deserted the ring to join the colors. But not Pete Herman! He just went on fighting. People began to ask all sorts of embarrassing questions. How come a fighting champ like Pete Herman wasn't in uniform? Why was he out of the biggest battle of them all?

The fingers began to point accusingly at Pete Herman. From jeers and whispers and laughter, the fans turned to a stronger way of showing their resentment. They began to boycott his fights. No one showed up when Pete went into the ring.

Little Pete Herman took it all without a whimper. He did not offer any public defense of his actions but continued calmly on his way, fighting as best he could, keeping his own counsel.

The war ended, and Pete was still in the ring. By this time he was a marked man, branded with the stigma of shame as a slacker.

Then the story finally came out. Pete fought his last fight a couple of years after the war ended and the referee, although giving him the decision, accused him of stalling because he missed so many punches. In quitting the ring, Pete told the story that only he and his manager knew—and the United States Navy. Pete had tried to enlist several times but each time had been rejected because he was blind in one eye and fast losing the sight of the other. Pete had pleaded with Navy officials to keep the secret, for, had the truth come out, Pete would have been finished as a fighter!

The secret of his partial blindness was well kept and Pete went on fighting through the war years in spite of the criticism heaped on him. Shortly after his last fight, Pete became totally blind. Now the little man, first New Orleans fighter ever to win a world's championship, runs a tavern in the French Quarter of his home city and dreams of the days when he was a champion and kept the secret of his blindness from the whole world!

MAMA'S BOY

The original "Mama's Boy" of the ring was Benny Leonard, that wizard with the gloves who retired as lightweight champion of the world, undefeated after an outstanding career. In an era of great lightweights, Benny shone like a meteor, beating the best and toughest fighters in the world.

Leonard came by his tag as a Mama's Boy honestly. It was no publicity stunt. Benny was very devoted to his mother who trembled with fear and concern every time her son had to enter the ring. He never fought anywhere without rushing to the phone the minute the bout was over to tell his beloved mother, "Hello, ma. I won and I'm not hurt a bit."

He was just an unknown kid from the sidewalks of New York when the shrewd boxing manager, Billy Gibson, bought up his contract for the sum of exactly one buck. It was the best investment Gibson ever made, for Leonard earned more than a million dollars with his flashy fists.

Benny showed his mother very soon that she had little to worry about when her darling boy entered the ring. He ran through the lightweight class like a cyclone. And, on a historic night in 1914, Benny met the world's champion, Freddy Welsh, and knocked him out in the ninth round.

Thus began a glorious fistic reign for the new lightweight champion. He was great in victory, but he was just as great when defeat stared him in the face. One time,

Lew Tendler had him on the ropes, groggy and beaten. Another punch and Leonard would have been shorn of his crown. But the clever champion grinned contemptuously at the eager challenger and whispered in his ear as they went into a clinch, "Can't you hit any harder than that?" Tendler, rattled by the taunt, hesitated. The blow he was about to throw remained poised in mid-air. And the challenger's chance vanished with his hesitation. Benny quickly recovered and went on to win the fight, saving his crown.

How great a fighter Leonard was can be indicated by one of the cute tricks he was noted for in his heyday. He always came into a fight with his hair carefully slicked down. The pretty hair-do was a constant challenge to his opponents, but Benny usually left the ring at the end of the fight with every hair in exactly the same place it had been at the beginning of the fight.

For eight long years, Benny Leonard ruled the lightweight class. Then, having run out of opponents, he did what made his mother the happiest woman in the world. He retired from the ring, an undefeated champion.

When Benny hung up his gloves for good his friends wondered whether he meant to quit the ring altogether. "Oh, no," he said, "I'll be in boxing till I breathe my last."

Benny Leonard kept his word better than he realized. He became an outstanding official. Then, when only 51, in the middle of an exciting bout that he was refereeing, Benny Leonard died where he had fought so many fights —in the center of the ring!

THE STORY BEGINS ON AN UGLY NOTE. ONE NIGHT, NOT TOO many years ago, Papa Rosofsky, a kind and meek little man, sat all alone in his grocery store in the slum section of Chicago. Two men walked in brandishing pistols.

A moment later, there was a shot and Papa Rosofsky fell dead. The gunmen scooped up the paltry contents of the cash register and fled into the night.

Papa Rosofsky's little boy, Barney, was only a high school youngster when his father was brutally murdered. There was a grief-stricken mother and a number of little brothers and sisters who had to be fed. So 14-year-old Barney quit school to become the breadwinner of the family. He sold newspapers on street corners; he shined shoes.

The kid was handy with his fists and it was lucky for him because he had to do his share of street-brawling to get by. Impatient with the meagre return from newspaper-selling, Barney decided to try the ring professionally.

Mama Rosofsky was dead set against her boy's ambition. She was a simple religious woman who knew nothing about the world of fisticuffs. When Barney came to her with his plans, he said to her, "Mama, I'll be a champion one day, and you'll have a beautiful fur coat to keep you warm and a nice house to live in."

Mama Rosofsky's eyes filled with tears. "Better I should walk the rest of my life in rags," she replied, "and live in a hovel, than to see you hurt."

But Barney was determined, and regretfully, Mama Rosofsky gave in. With her own hands she sewed the first pair of boxing trunks he wore in the ring.

The first thing young Barney did was get himself a new name for the ring. He did it very simply by shortening his last name. He became Barney Ross.

Once she had given her consent, Barney's mother helped her boy in every way she could. She cooked his meals in training camps, tucked him into bed, watched over him. Often, when the sledding was tough, it was Mama Ross who always said, "I believe in you, Barney. You will be a champion, I know it."

As a fighter, Barney Ross proved himself a battler with genuine class. From preliminary fights he went on to six-rounders, then to semi-final bouts and finally to the big time. Before long, Barney Ross became the light-weight champion of the world after beating Tony Canzoneri in fifteen cruel and bloody rounds.

He won greater honors and acclaim. A credit to boxing, and a great fighter who never ducked an opponent, Barney Ross went on to add the welterweight championship of the world to his other title.

At the crest of his fame, with a fortune earned in the ring, and with the respect and love of all fight fans, Barney Ross at last retired. No champion had ever more richly deserved the respect he held.

The years went by and little more was heard about Barney Ross, former lightweight and welterweight champion of the world. Then America went to war. Though he had streaks of grey in his hair, Barney Ross, well into his thirties, enlisted in the U. S. Marines. Little did he know that his greatest fight still lay before him.

It was on the island of Guadalcanal that Barney Ross met the stiffest test of his life. Against terrific odds, he found himself with three wounded comrades defending a foxhole against a horde of Japanese. All through a bitter night, Barney Ross stood guard over his wounded buddies. At dawn, he was relieved by U. S. Army reinforcements.

For his bravery in that bloody battle, Barney Ross was decorated with the Distinguished Service Cross, the Silver Star, and a Presidential Citation.

It was a terrible ordeal that Barney Ross had gone through and it left him a sick and broken man. Then, one day in 1948, worried fight fans heard a startling story about the former champion. A new patient who had arrived at the U. S. Public Health Service Hospital at

Lexington, Kentucky, was identified as Barney Ross. Worried, ashamed, and crushed, the sick man was voluntarily surrendering himself to the Government for treatment of the drug habit acquired as a result of repeated attacks of malaria.

Still, no one doubted that the game little ex-champ would make it. It was not long before Barney Ross was well and whole again, completely freed of the need for drugs. Surely no fight fan ever read a headline that gave him a bigger kick than the one that appeared when Barney left the hospital.

"Barney Ross KO's Drug Habit!"

"Mama's Boy"—that grand little champion had never fought a better fight!

When tall, handsome Young Willie Stribling stepped into the challenger's corner ready to begin his fight for the heavyweight championship with Max Schmeling, all eyes turned to the space under the ring where the challenger's manager stood. As usual, it was Ma Stribling, mother of the boy from Georgia, Ma Stribling who had brought her son to this point after having planned it for twenty-five years.

Whatever the bout may have meant to the champion or to Young Stribling himself with his record of some 300 fights, no one questioned that it was Ma Stribling's dream come true at last. Almost from the day of his birth, William Lawrence Stribling had been meant for the prize ring. From earliest childhood, Ma instilled in her son's heart this dream of ring glory. The boy began to learn to box almost as soon as his little legs could hold him up.

It was Ma Stribling who took complete charge of her son and his boxing career. She bought him his first pair of tiny boxing gloves. Under her loving care the kid grew big and husky. He learned fast and was barely sixteen when he became a professional.

Ma Stribling became her son's manager, trainer, time-keeper, and chief rooter. She cooked his food. She watched him as he went through his training, nursed him and patched his wounds, criticized and advised him. In fight after fight, in tank towns and big cities, she was always at ringside, in her son's corner, stop watch in hand to time the rounds, a little bag in her lap containing cotton, argyrol, other medicines that might be needed. Win or lose, her face never changed expression.

Under Ma's influence, Young Willie Stribling became a first-class boxer. Before he was 21, he had fought in feature bouts against many of the best heavyweights in the world, and had more than held his own.

Ma Stribling's dream came true at last when her boy was matched with Max Schmeling, the heavyweight champion of the world. Her heart surged with pride as her handsome son bounded into the ring. But whatever she felt she kept to herself.

For the first four rounds of the battle, Willie traded blows with the rugged champion on fairly even terms. But as the sixth round began, the tide began to turn surely in the beetle-browed Max's favor. His cruel punches began to land with more and more frequency.

You couldn't tell by looking at Ma Stribling that the beating her boy was taking had any effect on her. Her lips compressed, her only thought was that her son had to win, no matter how.

Young Stribling fought on desperately, furiously. It was a hopeless struggle. Schmeling put an end to the bout only 14 seconds before the final bell. Stribling had taken a count of nine. His eyes bleary, his lips cut and his face swollen beyond recognition, he was lurching forward when the referee mercifully stopped the contest. It was

Stribling's first defeat by a knockout, in more than 300 fights.

Stribling staggered out of the ring and into the arms of his mother. The Spartan woman refused to let the gaping spectators see what must have been in her heart at this moment. She put her arms around her son's shoulders and kissed his gashed lips. Then, calmly, she said to him, "I'm sorry, son, that we failed."

Stribling brushed away his tears and tried to mumble some reply. Ma stopped him gently. She took his arm and, together, mother and son walked up the aisle to the dressing rooms.

It was the last time for Young Stribling. He never fought again after losing his bid for the championship. Ma Stribling had seen her dream of a lifetime shattered forever.

The story ends on a note of bitter irony. Young Stribling, created by a mother's love, lost his life because of another mother. Speeding recklessly on his motorcycle to his wife, who had just given birth to a son, Young Stribling, the man who nearly became a ring champ through a mother's dream, fell and was instantly killed.

A BLOODY AFTERNOON IN SPAIN

Many a fight ends in wild confusion but the palm must go to the wind-up of the battle between Primo Carnera and Paolino Uzcudun, in Barcelona, Spain, some years ago. Fight fans who usually take their sport seriously never ran into a situation like the one that took place that day.

It was on a Sunday afternoon that 140,000 fanatical spectators jammed the huge outdoor arena where the bout was scheduled to take place. It was the biggest crowd ever known to see a boxing match.

The fight was scheduled to begin at two-thirty. The appointed time came and went. Not a soul had appeared in the ring. The huge crowd began to stir with impatience. The atmosphere began to charge with ominous foreboding. Thousands of military police and soldiers were present, armed to the teeth.

Unknown to the great crowd, a drama of unusual significance was taking place in the fighters' dressing rooms. The president of the Spanish Boxing Federation had handed Carnera a brand new pair of boxing gloves for the contest. Carnera took one look at them and refused to put them on. He insisted that he would use only American-made gloves. There was a long and bitter argument.

Half an hour passed, an hour. Still the giant refused to give in. Finally the president of the Boxing Federation lost all patience. Shouting angrily that Carnera's refusal to wear Spanish gloves was an insult to the whole nation and its people, he rushed to the door and barked a sharp command. Into the dressing room burst several Spanish soldiers, their rifles cocked and ready. Another command and the rifles lowered ominously, aiming straight at the big broad chest of the Italian colossus.

"Señor Carnera," said the president of the Spanish Boxing Federation calmly, "you will use our boxing gloves or I will order these soldiers to shoot!"

Needless to say, Carnera immediately acquiesced. He drew on the gloves and left the dressing room without another word.

Once inside the ring another bitter argument took place. Primo refused to go ahead with the fight because both the referee and the two judges were Spanish. A compromise was effected. New appointments were made. There would be one Spanish judge, one Italian judge, and an English referee.

At last, the fight started. Paolino proceeded to slam the clumsy Carnera from pillar to post, winning every round of the contest. At the final bell, the Italian judge and the English referee hastily handed in their sealed verdicts and immediately rushed out of the arena to catch a plane.

When the announcer opened the sealed ballots, he almost collapsed with shock. Both men had given the decision to the badly beaten Carnera! There was nothing for him to do but make the announcement. Then the storm broke!

The fanatical fight mob went wild. Men stood and cursed, women wept and screamed. Bottles flew through the stands. Another minute passed, and knives began to flash in the bright sun. Rifle fire spluttered, pistols barked. Fans fired into the ranks of police, police and soldiers fired back at the mob.

The huge Primo Carnera quickly dove into the security offered by the space beneath the ring.

Above his head the battle raged on. It endured for nearly an hour. Then, suddenly, a stillness fell on the great arena. Primo Carnera waited another minute, then cautiously crawled out of his hiding place. He looked around him in wonder. Nothing moved in the huge amphitheatre. The place was deserted. All who could had left, but here and there on the ground and in the rows lay still bodies of men and women who had been shot. There were almost fifty dead and injured left behind in this strangest aftermath of any prize fight ever known in sports history.

FOR THE LOVE OF SOMEONE

In his time, Felix Distrito was a good fighter. He was a game brown-skinned little warrior who fought in the lightweight ranks and did very well. He may be forgotten today but no Christmas passes that I do not remember his story.

Felix was as happy as his name. He had money, a loving wife, and a darling little daughter. Then tragedy struck at Felix Distrito. His eyes began to go back on him. At first he did not tell his wife about it. But as things became dimmer and dimmer, Felix found that he could no longer hide his secret. He was going blind. All the fights he had had, the cruel blows he had taken in the ring, were slowly but surely taking their toll. Before long, Felix was blind.

To get about, Felix bought himself a beautiful police dog named Queenie. Queenie was the eyes of the blind prize fighter. Wherever the blind man went, Queenie was at his side to guide his footsteps.

His money ran out, and in order to live, Felix found a job peddling peanuts in the very sport arena where once he had starred as a fighter. Blind Felix Distrito and his faithful dog, Queenie, became a familiar sight to sportswriters, boxers, and even to fans of the game.

Before Christmas his child took sick. Felix did not leave her bedside. Queenie too stood by her master, waiting and watching with almost human understanding. There was no money for food, no money for doctors, medicine, for anything that could help the ailing child.

One night, as Felix sat helplessly by his feverish daughter's bedside, an odd thing happened. Queenie suddenly rose from the corner in which she was lying and crossed the room to her master. She pressed her cold nose into his hand. Felix felt that the dog was trying to say something. He strained to understand her for a long minute. Then, without a word, he put on his shabby hat and coat and left the house.

Felix went to a local radio station accompanied by his faithful companion, sought out the sports announcer and told him his story. "Go on the air, please," begged Felix. "Offer Queenie for sale. Tell them what a fine dog she is. If I can't sell her my little girl will die because I haven't any money for food or medicine or a doctor."

"How will you get along without the dog?" asked the announcer.

"That doesn't matter," said Felix gently. "It's Queenie's own idea that I should sell her. I know because she told me."

That night an appeal went over the air. The appeal was not for someone to buy Queenie. It was an appeal for help for a courageous blind prize fighter who was willing to sell his eyes so that his child might live.

The appeal, made as it was in the Christmas season, touched the heart of a city. Money poured in from all sources. . . fight fans, hardboiled boxing managers, prize-fighters, even from plain ordinary citizens who had never seen a fight. Enough came in to pay the bills and to send the sick little girl to a fine hospital for treatment. Most important of all, the response of the public made it possible for Felix and Queenie to stay together. It was indeed a merry Christmas for a blind man, his sick child, and his faithful and loving "eyes," Queenie!

BACK IN 1931, A YOUNG BANTAMWEIGHT, GEORGIE GOOD-man by name, was plowing his way through the amateur ranks in the city of Chicago. Seasoned observers predicted a bright future for the fighting kid when he turned pro soon after.

The ring-wise gentry weren't mistaken. He began to move up and up in the professional ranks, blazing a trail with his fists that would surely lead to the championship. Then something happened just as George was to be matched for the title with the champion of the bantam-weight division. He fell in love, got married, and quit the ring.

About ten years later a tired, worried-looking little man entered the office of Charley McDonald, promoter of fights in the Hollywood Legion Stadium. With astonishment, the promoter recognized the once sensational bantam. Humble and shame-faced, the ex-fighter poured out a heart-breaking story. He had to have a fight. The promoter shook his head dubiously. "I'd like to give you a break, kid," he said. "But just look at yourself. You're in no shape to fight. You're washed up!"

The ex-fighter shivered. With tears in his eyes, he began to plead. "I'm not worrying about myself," he said. "I expect to take a beating, but I can't help it! I won't lie down now. I'll give the customers a run for their money, I promise! Please give me a fight! I need the dough; my wife's dying and she needs an immediate operation."

Finally the promoter yielded. A few days later he ar-ranged a match for the desperate man. Without a chance to get himself into any kind of shape for the bout, the former fighter climbed into the ring. He was only to go four rounds in a preliminary bout against Peppy Sanchez, whom he had fought years before, and whom he had then beaten decisively. Georgie Goodman knew what to expect. Sanchez would be out to get revenge for that defeat.

But the kid didn't care. How could he when he was fighting for his wife's life? He came out of his corner at the bell, his mind dazed, his thoughts anywhere but on the fight before him. No matter where he looked he could see only a far-off hospital room in which his wife lay dying.

Just the same, Georgie Goodman got in the first blow. The two men sparred cautiously a while. Then Sanchez saw an opening in his opponent's feeble guard and poured in some hot leather. Goodman rocked on his heels and fell back, his right cheek ripped open. He stuck out the round, rested briefly in his corner and came out for the second round. Sanchez was more than ready for him. He punched Georgie from pillar to post. At the bell, Goodman was groggy but still on his feet. The third round was a replica of the first, bloodier if possible. Sanchez dropped him for a short count. Georgie staggered to his feet, his numbed brain urging him on, telling him he had never been knocked out in his life. The fourth round was torture both to the beaten fighter and the crowd that watched this exhibition of raw courage. The final bell was more welcome to the onlookers than to Goodman.

As soon as the bout was over, Georgie Goodman staggered from the ring, collected his $125 and rushed to the hospital to see the doctor. He hardly felt his bruises in the thought that now at last his wife could have her operation. What did it matter that she would not approve of the fact that he had fought in the ring to get the money to pay for it?

Georgie Goodman's wife had her operation, all right, but unlike the usual Hollywood finish, it wasn't a success. For a few hours all went well. Then the fighter's wife died. Georgie Goodman sat dazed and dull, his eyes fixed on space unseeingly. Then at dawn he got up and went home.

The papers carried the story that morning. It wasn't much of a story so they only gave it a couple of lines. They read like this:

"Peppy Sanchez beat Georgie Goodman last night by a decision in four rounds."

A SENTIMENTAL OLDTIMER TOLD ME THIS TALE. I DOUBT IF it's true. But it's a sweet yarn, so take it for what it's worth to your heart.

Perhaps you've never heard of the prize fighter, Swifty Jones. His name never appeared in any headlines. He fought in the ring about forty years ago. At best, he was just a third-rater, one of those hopeless stumble-bums who fight for coffee-and-cake money in dingy little boxing clubs. However, there's a story to be told about him, and it's a tale best told around Christmas time.

After years of battling in the ring, serving as a human punching bag for every up-and-coming youngster on the way to fistic fame, Swifty Jones seemed to have reached the end of the trail. To get fights became increasingly hard for him. When he begged a promoter for a match, the reply would always be:

"Beat it, Swifty, I ain't got nuthin' for you. I don't want any guy to get killed in my place. Why don't you hang up your gloves? You're through." And Swifty Jones would just shrug his shoulders and go his way.

Some days before Christmas, Swifty went walking with his wife. She happened to see a beautiful white dress in a shop window.

"Swifty," she exclaimed, "wouldn't it be wonderful if I could wear a dress like that again for Christmas?"

Swifty just nodded his head but in his heart there was pain. More than anything else in the world, he wanted his wife's wish to come true. And Swifty determined to get the money to buy that beautiful white dress for his wife to wear on Christmas Eve.

The next few days, Swifty went frantically from promoter to promoter, but they all turned him down. Finally, as he was being turned down for the tenth time, a matchmaker suddenly said:

"Wait a minute, Swifty, I've got a fight for you if you want to do business. I've got a green kid comin' up. I want him to make a great showing in my club tonight . . . Christmas Eve spirit, you know. Now, if you go out in the second round, there'll be thirty bucks in it for you. Wanna take it?"

For a moment, Swifty ached to take a poke at the man. All his life, win or lose, he had never fought a crooked fight. He had sunk low, but not low enough to throw a fight. Then suddenly, a voice inside of him began to whisper:

"Oh, Swifty, what a beautiful white dress. Wouldn't it be wonderful if I could wear a dress like that for Christmas?" Swifty Jones took that fight. He came home that afternoon, plunked down thirty dollars before his wife's surprised eyes and said:

"Honey, I'm fightin' tonight. Here's the money. G'wan and buy yourself that beautiful white dress. It's my Christmas present to you. Remember, when I come home tonight, I want to see you wearin' that beautiful white dress. It'll be Christmas Eve."

That night, Swifty climbed through the ropes to fight the green youngster. In the first minute of that battle, he realized that if he had only wanted, he could win the bout with ease. But he had made a bargain. And so, in the second round, Swifty took a punch on the chin and went down and was counted out.

Quickly, he dressed and left the arena. It was Christmas Eve and he felt ashamed of himself. He had thrown a fight. However, he felt a little better when he remembered that at home, his wife would greet him wearing that beautiful white dress. But as he entered his shabby room, his wife met him at the door with tears in her eyes. And she wasn't wearing the beautiful white dress. She was wearing her old frayed one.

"Swifty," she cried, "You lost the fight, and I thought you would win. I had faith in you."

"What's that got to do with my winnin' or losin'? I gave you the thirty bucks to buy a dress," growled Swifty. "Why didn't you do it?"

Sobbing, his wife replied:

"Because I wanted to buy a Christmas present for you, too. So I bet the thirty dollars that you'd win. Now we lost everything and it's all my fault."

Swifty looked at his wife in a strange way. He wanted to tell her how low he had sunk, how ironic it all was. Here, he had agreed to throw a fight for the first time in his life, and for the first time in her life, his wife had bet on him. That was retribution. Yes, all those things Swifty wanted to tell his sobbing wife. But all he did was to take her in his arms, kiss her, and softly say:

"Merry Christmas, dear!"

A BLOODY NOSE FOR YOUR TROUBLE

Many years ago there lived a fighter famed far and wide as the Nonpareil, the original Jack Dempsey, middleweight champion of the world. While in San Francisco one day, he dropped into the gymnasium of an exclusive athletic club for a workout.

Unable to find a sparring partner, the Nonpareil sought out the boxing champion of the club and asked him whether he would care to go a few rounds with him. The club champion was a tall slim dignified-looking bank clerk.

The invitation from the great champion awed the young man but he eagerly accepted the challenge. It was an opportunity not to be missed, not even by an amateur.

For a while the two men sparred easily with the amateur holding his own against the middleweight champion. Then, suddenly, the Nonpareil brought up a hard right flush to the generously proportioned nose of his adversary.

The blood gushed from the wounded member. Fists swinging wildly, the young man lost his head and sailed into the great Nonpareil, determined to reduce him to powder.

The champion cleverly sidestepped, clinched, and pinned his opponent's arms to his sides. "Cool off, son," he whispered soothingly, "I'm sorry I gave you a bloody nose. Come on, let's be friends."

The words calmed the amateur quickly. He left the

floor for the dressing room and began to change. A few minutes later the Nonpareil joined him and threw a fatherly arm around his shoulders. "You're not a bad fighter, son," he said. "You have the spark of a champion. Take my advice and go into the ring. I'm sure there's a great future ahead of you. I'll help you all I can."

The two men became fast friends. They boxed together often and the eager young amateur learned all that the Nonpareil could teach him of the art of fisticuffs.

The boy was an apt and willing pupil. So well did he learn his chosen trade that, in time, he burst upon the sports world with a new kind of boxing magic, the cleverest boxer yet seen among the heavy men of the ring.

The day came when the former bank clerk flung out his dramatic challenge to the champion of the world—John L. Sullivan! His impudence was met by jeers, laughter and abuse. This dancing master, this dude, this softie, in the same ring with the great John L? Ridiculous!

In twenty-one bloody rounds, the challenger stabbed and parried, till the champion's face was a bloody mess. Finally the grand old champion went down, knocked out by the young upstart.

And it was a bloody nose that led the dignified young bank clerk to that moment in the ring that is every fighter's goal—the cry of the announcer when the champion has sunk into the dust of defeat: "The winner and new champion—James J. Corbett!"

THIS IS THE STORY OF A MAN WITH A BASHED-IN NOSE. HE was a prize fighter who wanted to be a champion. Though he failed in his ambition and became a laughingstock in the ring, time wrote a curious ending to his story.

Many years ago, Mike Carr was an up-and-coming welterweight. He could box, he could hit, he was game. Beginning as an unknown preliminary fighter, Mike Carr became a sensation. He fought the best of them, winning every time. Everyone was saying that nothing could stop Mike Carr from reaching the top. The man who believed it most of all was Mike Carr himself.

Then, one night, Mike met a tough opponent. He was far ahead on points, when suddenly he received a terrific blow right between the eyes. The punch almost broke his nose. Mike won the fight, and was rushed to the hospital for treatment. He returned to the ring, but somehow, he was never again the fighter he had been. Now, he was more cautious. He had lost his fire, and he began to lose fights he would have won easily before he was hurt.

One night, Mike Carr failed to show up for an important match. He just disappeared. When he was found weeks later he told his manager that he had decided to quit the ring forever.

"What are you going to do now?" asked his manager.

"I'm going to write songs," answered Mike.

The manager threw back his head and roared with laughter. "You're balmy, Mike!" he gasped. "You're out of your mind! Your place is in the ring, my boy. Why you've never written a song in your life!"

Mike shook his head.

"I don't care what you say. I'm going to write songs—songs about cowboys and the beautiful peaceful Golden West. No more fights for me."

Mike Carr was as good as his word. He never fought again. When the sports world heard that Mike Carr had quit the ring to write lyrics, they laughed and laughed.

A few stopped when Mike Carr became known as the author of a beautiful and melancholy song that went, in part, like this:

*"Ole Faithful, we rode the range together,
Ole Faithful, in every kind of weather,
When your round-up days are over
There'll be pastures white with clover
For you, Ole Faithful, pal o' mine."

There were still many who found amusement in the fighter turned songwriter. Suppose he had written a popular song? He couldn't do it again.

But Mike Carr did do it again.

Remember the song that went like this? . . . . .

†"South of the Border, down Mexico Way,
That's where I fell in love
When the stars above came out to play.
And now as I wander, my thoughts ever stray
South of the Border, down Mexico Way."

Down through the years, Mike Carr, the ex-prize fighter, continued writing beautiful melodies. His are the most popular cowboy songs ever written. It was certainly a strange metamorphosis for a prize fighter, but that is not the strangest part of the story. The most amazing thing is that Mike Carr, the prize fighter who gave up a career in the ring to write songs of the Golden West, is an Englishman who has never been in the United States and never has seen a live cowboy!

FIFTY GRAND

Comes February or March every year, and a tiny item squeezes itself into the sports pages. If you read your favorite newspaper carefully you won't miss it. It will usually say, "Harry Wills, former great heavyweight fighter, began his fast today." To the fight fan the story is a familiar one since it has been repeated each year for nearly forty years. Harry Wills, now close to sixty, has not varied this one procedure in all his adult life.

Harry fasts for thirty days each year and drops some sixty pounds in the process. He says it makes him feel fine, and anyone seeing the tall powerful Negro striding down the street would attest to that. He looks, even today, as though he's in shape to challenge the champion for the title.

But Harry Wills is no longer interested in the ring. He has made his pile and is living comfortably on his income. He did quite well as a fighter but no purse ever came more easily to him than the $50,000 he once received —for not fighting at all! Here is how it happened.

Jack Dempsey was the heavyweight champion of the world. There wasn't a man around who was given half a chance of licking the great Manassa Mauler. Then, one day, a huge powerful giant by the name of Harry Wills showed up on the fistic scene and began to bowl over the best heavyweights in America. Before long, he challenged the great Dempsey to fight for the title.

For some reason or other, the Manassa Mauler saw fit to ignore him. With every winning fight, Harry Wills repeated his challenge. For years, he shadowed the champion, begging, pleading, demanding a match. Rumors flew thick and fast concerning the reasons for the match not being made. One of the most popular beliefs was that a meeting between Wills and Dempsey would cause riots and a national scandal. Others thought that Dempsey feared the big challenger.

Although Dempsey denied all accusations and ridiculed the skeptics who doubted that he could lick anyone alive, he continued to avoid Harry Wills. And, as Wills continued to win fight after fight, it became increasingly difficult for the champion to sidestep him.

Finally, Dempsey was cornered. A syndicate of sportsmen made an offer too tempting to refuse and articles were signed. Dempsey was guaranteed a huge sum as his end. But he was obliged to put up a $50,000 forfeit to be paid the challenger if, for any reason, the fight did not take place as scheduled.

Both men went into serious training. The whole country began to sizzle about the approaching battle. Then another flock of rumors began to pop. One had it that Dempsey was ill. Another held that trouble would be sure to start if the two men went through with the fight. A third, and more persistent one, said that powerful forces were pulling strings to keep the fight from taking place. The public had faith in the Manassa Mauler and was sure the two men would go through with the contest as scheduled.

At the last minute, the bout was called off. Who gave the order, why it was given, no one knew. Dempsey said nothing, Wills said less. Harry Wills quietly collected the $50,000 that was his in forfeit and went home, never to challenge the champion again.

Since Harry Wills and Sam Langford met fourteen times in the ring to create one of the longest series in boxing history, it is fitting to spin a tale of Langford which curiously enough, was also staged in a $50,000 setting.

Boxing fans were shaken to their heels one day several years ago when a New York reporter, acting on a tip, rushed up to Harlem and found one of the greatest of all heavyweight fighters blind, broke and practically forgotten by everyone. The great oldtimer was Sam Langford, one of the legendary figures of the ring, now reduced to wondering where and how he could scrape up the buck and a half he needed each week to keep a roof over his head.

As he sat staring hopelessly into space, it is possible that from time to time memories of the past crowded into his mind. If they did, it is certain that among them was a certain incident from the dim past when Sam Langford, in England for one of his fights, made one of the biggest bets ever placed on a fight.

Back in 1909, Sam Langford, better known as the "Boston Tar Baby," was the uncrowned heavyweight champion of the world in the eyes of his affectionate admirers. Champions ducked him like the plague. Many of the fights he did get were based on his promise solemnly given not to do his best against his opponent. Since most heavies of the time feared the powerful and clever Langford, pickings were few and far between.

One day an offer came from England to fight a highly-touted favorite named Iron Hague. Offered ten thousand dollars and expenses to make the trip, Langford and his manager, Joe Woodman, almost fell over each other in their rush to the telegraph office to wire their acceptance. It didn't matter to them that Iron Hague had ripped his way through all the heavyweights in England and was considered a great fighter over there. Langford was supremely confident that he could lick anyone who would step into the ring with him.

A few hours before the fight was to start, Langford decided to bet his end of the purse on himself to win. The price was even money. Though neither manager nor fighter had the actual cash, since the purse had not yet been collected, the bet could be made under English custom where an oral wager was acceptable, provided a man's credit was good.

Woodman went off immediately to the leading pub where all the sportsmen congregated. Stepping up to the bar, he slapped his passport and identification papers down on the mahogany and shouted for all to hear, "I want to bet ten thousand on Langford!"

The bet was snatched up quickly. Sticking the slip recording the wager into his pocket, Woodman left the bar to rejoin Langford. However, he lost his way in the twisting London streets. He did not reach Langford until the great fighter was walking down the aisle towards the ring. Quickly, Woodman climbed into his man's corner, rolled up his sleeves and prepared to guide Langford to the victory of which they were so confident.

Woodman yanked the betting slip out of his pocket and waved it before Sam Langford's face. "Here it is!" he shouted above the din. "The bet's down, Sam! Ten thousand on you at even money!"

Sam Langford looked at the bit of paper and his eyes almost popped out of his head. "Hey!" he yelled. "Look what you gone and done! If I don't win this fight tonight, we lose $50,000! We ain't got that kind of money, Joe! We'll go to jail if we can't pay it!"

"What are you blabbing about, man?" asked the puzzled Woodman. "How can we lose fifty grand when I only bet ten?"

Langford pushed the ticket under his manager's nose.

"Look for yourself," he said hoarsely. "The ticket says ten thousand—pounds! That's what you bet. And ten thousand pounds means fifty thousand in American money!"

Manager Woodman took a close look at the ticket and then the blood went clear out of his face. He fell into a dead faint, toppling right into the arms of Langford's handlers. They dragged the unconscious man out of the ring and went to work feverishly trying to revive him. In the midst of the confusion, the bell sounded. The fight was about to begin!

Sam Langford went to the center of the ring in a complete state of panic. Forgotten was the task before him. All he could think of was the fifty thousand. Suppose he should break some English rule he didn't know and be disqualified on the spot? Suppose—bang! Iron Hague had stepped forward and let fly at the petrified Langford's jaw. Langford wavered, his hands at his sides. Suppose—bang! Langford shook his head. "Where will I get the money if I lose?" he murmured. Bang! "I'm going to jail sure as shooting if I lose this fight," thought Langford to himself.

For three rounds, Iron Hague battered Langford from pillar to post as the American tried to figure out what to do about the bet his manager had made. Meanwhile, that worthy still lay sprawled outside the ring, dead to the world.

In the last seconds of the third round, Iron Hague landed a haymaker on Langford's chin that brought a most unusual reaction in its train. Instead of putting the "Boston Tar Baby" to sleep as might have been expected, it did just the opposite. Langford, who had been fighting as though in a daze, suddenly came to his senses. In the fourth round, Langford momentarily hooked Iron Hague's arms in a clinch and whispered in his ear,

"I'm sorry, fellow, but I got to do it. This worrying is just about killing me!" Stepping back from the clinch, Langford let fly a tremendous punch. Iron Hague fell as though poleaxed. The referee started to count ten, but he could just as easily have counted ten thousand. Sam took one look at the recumbent figure and then turned his back to it, walked to his corner and leaned over the ropes, peering anxiously down towards his unconscious manager. He shook his head and then grinned.

"Hey, boss!" he shouted at the top of his lungs. "You can wake up now! I've won! We ain't going to no jail!"

The next day Sam Langford collected fifty thousand dollars at the barroom, put it with the ten thousand that was his end of the purse, and sailed back home. The trip had been a very profitable one, to be sure, as well as a lesson in foreign exchange to his manager.

It could be that the story, if remembered by the blind and lonely old man, is still good for a chuckle in the dark hours of waiting in that shabby furnished room. But where does a guy get a buck and a half for this week's room rent? That's more important to Sam Langford than a memory, more urgent than the best laugh he ever had.

PRIDE AND GALL

Every time I think of Max Schmeling accepting the heavy-weight crown while sitting more or less uncomfortably on the seat of his pants, it puts me in mind of a famous old-time boxing man who refused the title because he couldn't win it fair and square by fighting for it.

It was in the gay and golden 90s that the American boxing world was invaded by a proud and fighting Irishman named Peter Maher. Although he wasn't more than a light-heavyweight, as measured by the scales, Peter Maher licked every big man who dared to crawl through the ropes to face him. Some of the greatest of them all were campaigning at that time, immortals like Bob Fitzsimmons, Jim Corbett, James Jeffries. Unfortunately, Maher never fought any of these ring greats while they held the title.

Peter Maher was at the peak of his form in 1892, and Gentleman Jim Corbett was champion of the world. The champion, who had been the first to destroy the John L. Sullivan myth, feared no man alive, but he was shrewd enough to know that the devastating wallop in the fists of Peter Maher were better avoided if possible. He refused point-blank to meet him.

In order to escape the insistent Maher, champion Jim Corbett took under his wing a tough young heavyweight fighter by the name of Steve O'Donnell. He intended to announce his retirement from the ring and he was grooming his protégé, O'Donnell, to take his place as champion.

When word of Corbett's intentions came to Peter Maher, he was furious. Publicly and loudly, he demanded the opportunity of meeting the champion in a title bout. Corbett was adamant. He insisted that he was going to retire from the ring, and that another man was to take his place.

However, the demand went up that Steve O'Donnell fight for the crown rather than accept it as a gift from a retiring champion. Jim Corbett finally succumbed to the pressure and consented to let his protégé fight to prove that he would be a worthy successor to the great Gentleman Jim. Peter Maher maneuvered himself into the picture as O'Donnell's opponent.

So sure of himself was the red-eyed Irishman that he bet his entire purse that he would knock out Corbett's man. No one ever had a surer wager. At the opening bell, Peter Maher flung himself across the ring at the hapless O'Donnell and stopped him in the very first round.

After the knockout, the embarrassed champion, Jim Corbett, stepped slowly into the center of the ring, raised his hand for silence and said, "I was wrong. Peter Maher is a great fighter. Now that I plan to retire, I have the honor of presenting him with my title."

Maher had only to nod his head to become world's heavyweight champion. The nod was not forthcoming. Stepping forward, Maher lifted his head and stared Corbett right in the eye. Then, in a booming voice that could be heard all over the arena, he shouted, "No! I want to be champion all right, but I don't want it this way. I want to fight for it. What's more, I want to win the title from the champion himself, not his stooge!"

The crowd sat stunned as Peter Maher, his head high, his proud eyes flashing, walked out of the ring. Peter Maher, for those few minutes, was truly a champion among champions. As for the title itself, he never managed to fight for it. For years, the Irish champion chased Corbett for a crack at the crown but without success. It was after his best fighting days were over that Peter Maher finally succeeded in making a match with Bob Fitzsimmons that was supposed to serve as an elimination bout with the winner meeting Corbett, the champion. By then it was too late. Fitz stopped Maher in a round, thus bringing to an end a glorious career that was never rewarded with the only prize worth having.

A FEW YEARS BACK THERE WAS A SMALL-TIME FIGHTER NAMED Al Simms who fought around the small clubs for nickels and dimes. Simms, a Negro lightweight, never did anything noteworthy in the ring. His only virtue as a fighter was his ability to take punishment and come back for more. You could call him a human punching bag and not be too far off the mark.

At 34, Simms' face was a shapeless lump that had been pounded and kneaded by ten thousand blows. His ears resembled a pair of pincushions, his nose was a boneless ripple, his eyes were deep-sunken in pads of scar-tissue. He wasn't very pretty, this mediocre lightweight, and no one knew it better than Al Simms himself.

One night Al crawled through the ropes in the stuffy St. Nicholas boxing arena in New York. Only two kinds of fighters appeared in old St. Nick's—the guy who was on his way out and the up and coming youngsters heading for the big time. The place was jammed to the rafters with some three thousand fight fans who had come to see the main go in which Simms was to play trial horse for a promising 19-year-old youngster who already bore the mark of a champion.

When Al Simms was introduced to the crowd, the mob howled and booed. This was nothing unusual. Simms bowed and smiled, nodding to right and left as the razzing grew in volume. The crowd which had come to see the youngster and not Simms, resented the Negro's friendly acceptance of their acclaim for the boy in the other corner. Fortunately the bell to start the bout put an end to the demonstration from the arena.

As soon as the fight started, the right hook that was to win a championship began to bang away at Al Simms' lumpy face. From every blow, every flurry of punches, the old has-been came back with a broad grin on his homely map. This grin annoyed the crowd and the booing for Al Simms grew louder and louder. In a short time they began to yell for blood. "Murder the bum! Knock 'im out!"

Al Simms took a brutal beating as the youngster, spurred on by the crowd, redoubled his efforts. Nevertheless, when the final bell sounded, Simms was still on his feet, shaky but still grinning that foolish grin. The decision was quickly awarded to his opponent. There could be no question as to who had won the fight. One had only to look at the two in the ring and compare the fresh unmarked youth with the badly beaten, bleeding and bruised Al Simms.

Suddenly, as the crowd prepared to leave, the announcer called for attention and silence. He said that Al Simms wished to make a statement to the crowd before leaving the ring. Puzzled, the crowd held fast and looked up in wonder as the beaten Negro, the mechanical grin still on his lips, tottered to the center of the ring. For a few seconds he just stood there and surveyed the crowd that had booed him so lustily all through the fight. Then the tears began to run from his eyes. He swallowed convulsively. Then he began to speak—the first time he had ever said a word in fifteen years of fighting in the prize ring.

"Gentlemen," he said, his voice carrying in the stillness

to the farthest corners of the smoke-filled club, "he didn't knock me down. The kid here's a good fighter, but he couldn't knock me down. You all saw it. Not once did he drop me. Well, anyway, folks, I'm glad you liked my fight, because it was my last one, see? I'm retiring from the ring. And I wish to take this occasion to thank you all for how kind you been to me all through my career. And honest, folks, I'll never forget you, and how you always gave a fellow a break and how you liked my efforts. Well, that's all. So long, everybody. And thanks! And remember, he didn't knock me down, no, sir! I finished on my feet!"

Al Simms brushed away his tears and turned away quickly from the microphone. Then, throwing back his shoulders, he made his way out of the ring, not like a beaten, punch-drunk palooka, but like a proud and dignified man, like a champion! His head high, Al Simms walked down the aisle towards the distant dressing rooms.

For a few minutes, the crowd sat in silence. Then, suddenly, from a distant corner of the arena, a cry went up from a single throat. "Atta boy, Al!"

Immediately other voices rose. Soon the room was filled with shouting voices and the loud clapping of hands. A terrific series of cheers rent the air as Al Simms hesitated before disappearing, smiled and raised his hands in grateful acknowledgement, then blew a farewell kiss to the crowd that had given him the first—and last—ovation of his career. In that magic moment was forgotten all the bitterness and pain and disappointment of a long and mediocre fighting career.

WHEN THE STARTLING NEWS REACHED THE TOWN OF SAPULpa, Oklahoma, that Jack Johnson had knocked out Jim Jeffries, and was now the heavyweight champion of the world, no man was more affected than a certain railroad engineer by the name of Carl Morris. Climbing down from the cab of his locomotive, big Carl announced, "Friends, I've just quit my job. I promise that I will never rest until I have beaten Johnson and restored the heavy-weight championship to the white race!" And, with tears streaming down his cheeks, the big fellow set forth to carry out his promise.

It didn't matter that big, clumsy, 240-pound Carl Morris had never worn a pair of boxing gloves in his life. Stories and pictures of this first of the "white hopes" filled the sports pages. What if he didn't know a thing about the art of boxing? The man was a strong giant and he was engaged in a holy cause.

In his footsteps, and on the same quest, followed other white hopes. Among them were sailors, bricklayers, steve-dores, hoboes, policemen, town loafers, lifeguards, butch-ers, bakers, and even candlestick makers. Few of them could fight, but all went gladly on the holy march to avenge good old Jim Jeffries and restore the title to the white race. Fight managers, with an eye for profit, played on the eagerness of these foolish young men. They pushed the clumsy hopefuls into rings from coast to coast. The white hopes returned, one by one, to their homes and old jobs, frightfully battered and punched out, convinced that the championship bubble was a will-o'-the-wisp.

But what of Carl Morris, the first, the original white hope? The man who had started the crusade was pushed into the ring like all the others. He fought a few minor contests with broken-down palookas until his ego was blown sky high by his phenomenal success. Then he was brought to New York and tossed into the ring at old Madison Square Garden with Jim Flynn, the Pueblo Fire-man.

It was a ridiculous sight to see both men climb through

the ropes. Morris was a giant who tipped the beam at 240 pounds. Flynn weighed barely 175 pounds. But Jim Flynn was a seasoned campaigner and one of the roughest and toughest heavyweights in the business.

With the first bell, Flynn began to batter the white hope from pillar to post. For ten long rounds, Flynn played so fierce a tattoo on clumsy Carl Morris that even the hard-boiled, bloodthirsty fans, moved either by pity or disgust, yelled for the referee to stop the slaughter. The arbiter ignored the pleas of the spectators and Morris himself refused to quit.

After this frightful beating, Carl Morris never was quite the same. He remained in the ring for some years, a shabby broken-down warrior, often losing. His purses got smaller and smaller, his body softer from the cruel beatings he took from every fifth-rater he met.

Meanwhile, among the other white hopes, sordid and tragic events were taking place. One by the name of Bull Young met Jess Willard, stepped into an uppercut from that future champ, and was killed. Another promising youngster named Luther McCarthy met his end in the ring from a blow in the neck. The crusade to restore the title to the white race was taking its toll!

And then Jess Willard won the title from Jack Johnson and the quest came to an end. It came to an end, that is, for everyone but big Carl Morris. The battered hulk of that once-magnificent man still hung on, still moved around the country, taking fearful beatings. Although a white man at last held the title, Carl refused point blank to quit. "I'm the original white hope," he would murmur, "I won't ever quit until I win the title and save it for the white race!"

In 1918, he met an ambitious youngster out of Manassa, Colorado, and was knocked out in one round. After he came to, the giant shook his head. "The kid was lucky to beat me," he mumbled. "He ain't a fighter, never will be one! Carl Morris will still be champ!"

But the career of Carl Morris was over, this time for good. Wrong as he was about his own goal, he was even more wrong about the kid who licked him. That kid went on to win the title himself and go down in history as the immortal Jack Dempsey!

AN AMUSING STORY CONCERNING SAM LANGFORD DEALS WITH that great fighter's brother. It seems that this brother, like most older brothers, considered himself a better fighter than Sam. One day, when Sam was visiting his family in his native Nova Scotia, he showed the folks some of the money he had earned in the ring.

Elder brother's eyes popped as he saw the thick pile of greenbacks. "Sure now, Sam," he said, "you ain't kidding, are you, when you say you get a couple of hundred of those dollars just for punching other boys?"

Sam grinned in reply and pulled another fistful of twenties out of his pocket. Elder brother shook his head in wonder at it all.

A few days after returning to Boston, Sam got the surprise of his life when his elder brother suddenly burst into his room in great excitement. "Here I am, Sam!" he announced. "Ain't no reason that I can see why two Langfords shouldn't make easy money!"

The next couple of months saw Sam Langford busy teaching his elder brother as much as he could of the science of boxing. After many hours of practice, elder brother finally became restless and insisted that it was high time he got his first crack at the real thing. Sam dutifully engineered a fight, selecting a particularly soft touch for the match.

The battle was a terrific one and elder brother took a

severe pasting from the palooka. By some miracle, the elder brother was handed a surprise decision at the end of the contest. Now he really began to puff up with importance. With a winning streak of one, elder brother was ready to meet the next obstacle on his climb to the championship. Despite Sam's advice to quit while the quitting was good, elder brother insisted on another match at once.

The fight was made, this time with a fifth-rater. In the first round, elder brother Langford was knocked down ten, count them, ten times. In the second round, he was knocked unconscious, a state in which he remained for almost an hour.

It was with difficulty that old Sam brought his brother to his senses at last. As the elder brother's eyes fluttered open, he looked up at Sam with a sad expression on his face. "Sam," he muttered, "you were right. I should have retired with my winning streak of one. This fighting business ain't good for the soul—and it sure ain't good for the body, either!"

When the aches and pains of his unfortunate experience had gone, elder brother made haste to join the church and become a preacher. From that time on, he tried to score knockouts only over the devil, leaving fighting in the ring to his brother, Sam. He never again brought up the old time boast that he was a better fighter than the great Sam Langford!

AT THE TURN OF THE CENTURY AN AMAZING CHARACTER APpeared in the ring. His name was Joe Grimm. He had no boxing skill and no punch, but he possessed an incredible ability to absorb punishment. At the beginning of every fight, he would walk over to the ropes and roar at the crowd:

"I am Joe Grimm! I fear no man alive!"

He fought every great heavyweight of his time, and they all whaled the daylights out of him. In every fight, iron man Joe Grimm would take the most brutal beatings imaginable, but at the end of every fight, he would stagger to the ropes and again roar at the crowd his familiar boast:

"I am Joe Grimm! I fear no man!"

It was in a match with the feared Bob Fitzsimmons during the days when Jim Jeffries was the heavyweight champion of the world, that Joe Grimm showed that he had an iron gall as well as an iron jaw.

When the bout with Grimm was proposed to Bob Fitzsimmons, the lanky Cornishman objected to meeting the Iron Man. "I know he can't hit or box," protested Ruby Bob. "It's just that I don't want to be breaking my hands on his head."

The promoter convinced Bob that the Iron Man had never met so hard a puncher as Fitzsimmons. "Besides," added the promoter, "that guy ought to be pretty well softened up for you after all the beatings he's taken."

Bob accepted the match, determined to show the world that he could do what no one else had been able to do—knock out the Iron Man, Joe Grimm.

As the bout started, Bob advanced across the ring, shifted slightly to one side, and let fly a deadly hook to the Iron Man's jaw. It was a blow as hard as Fitz had ever struck in his life, and he stepped back to give the Iron Man room to stretch out on the canvas. Joe went down with a thud and just as quickly bounced up again, fresh as a daisy.

Amazed at the other's recuperative power, Bob Fitzsimmons moved in again, jabbed with a left, and then brought up a terrific right cross that would have torn the head off a bull calf. Down went Joe Grimm—and up he bounced again, none the worse for wear.

Bob was puzzled now. And, being puzzled, he could

think of only one thing to do—and that was to keep on hitting and hitting until that exasperating man of iron did go down for good.

The bout was a six-rounder. The details of the fight are not important. What happened in the first round happened in the next and the next and the next. Fitzsimmons kneaded Joe Grimm like a ball of dough. The punches rattled off the Iron Man like hail from a tin roof. He went to the canvas a total of thirteen times in the short fight. The only sign that Joe was feeling the punishment was that he began to take a little more time getting up. Towards the end he was actually using the full nine seconds allowed under the rules.

At the very end, his face a crimson mess and both eyes closed, Joe Grimm was still groping around the ring looking for his opponent, following him from corner to corner, shedding blows that would have felled an ox. When the last bell sounded, Joe Grimm was still trying to hit the lanky Cornishman. Fitzsimmons, more in pity than disgust, was standing back out of reach.

There was polite applause for the winner, Bob Fitzsimmons, but there was a thunderous burst of cheering for the Iron Man. Grimm smiled through his cracked lips at the ovation he received. Then, lifting his weary arms in a signal calling for silence, he stepped back to the center of the ring.

"There's only one thing I want now!" he shouted. "I'd like to fight the champion, Jim Jeffries!"

There's no accounting for some fighters' gall!

NOT SO VERY LONG AGO, A POLICEMAN FOUND A SHABBY, bearded old beggar on a deserted dock along New York's waterfront. He was dead. Off to the morgue they carted him, just another hunk of human driftwood gathered in from the streets of a big city.

However, before they could bury that old beggar in a nameless grave in potter's field, it was discovered that he was Kid Broad, once known to ring fame as a great lightweight. In his day, Kid Broad fought immortals of the roped arena like Abe Attell, George Dixon, Jimmy Britt and Young Corbett, and no one ever dropped Kid Broad for the full count. There never lived a fighter with more amazing stamina than the incredible Kid Broad.

He was often knocked down by an opponent, but there was no one who could keep him down. Whenever he hit the canvas, the Kid used to give himself a pep talk, audible to many sitting at ringside. "Come on, Kid," he used to say. "Get up! You mustn't get yourself knocked out. Take a beating if you have to, but don't get knocked out. Your father back in Cleveland wouldn't like it!" And with those words, Kid Broad used to stagger to his feet and go on with the fight.

One day, however, the Kid was matched with Aurelio Herrerra, reputed to be the hardest hitter in the lightweight division. The first blow of the fight was a terrific smash to the jaw landed by the Mexican and Kid Broad went down. Badly shaken, he groped on all fours and began to mumble his usual pep talk to himself. "Come on, Kid, get up. Your father in Cleveland wouldn't like it if you lost this fight."

Kid Broad staggered to his feet and walked into another terrific blow. Again he went down. And again he talked himself to his feet.

The Kid took a terrible beating through the first four rounds. The fans marveled at his staying power. In the fifth round, the Mexican landed the hardest blow of the fight. Down went the Kid. Weakly he rolled over and raised himself to one knee, mumbling through bloody lips, "Get up, Kid, get up." As the fans held their breath, the Kid started to get up. But just as it seemed that he was going to make it again, he flopped back to the canvas, put a hand under his head like a pillow, and shouted angrily, "To hell with the old man in Cleveland! This crazy guy will kill me if I get up again!"

TOGETHER

It is believed that "Baby-face" Jimmy McLarnin was the best managed prize fighter who ever worked in the land of blood-and-brawl.

The team of Jimmy McLarnin and Pop Foster is now but a legend of bygone days, but baby-faced Jimmy and Pop knew how to stand together. That's the way they started back in the golden twenties, often hated, often loved, through poverty and fame, but always together. The world of sport knew them as fighter and manager. They were more like father and son.

The air was autumn-clear one day about twenty years ago when Pop Foster leaned down to tie his shoe and found fortune tangled in the laces. As he straightened up he glanced into the school yard before him and observed a game of leapfrog. One of the little fellows playing had the face of an angel and the legs of a young antelope. Pop watched the boy for a long time. He came back the next day and the next. Pop couldn't tell you why he did this. All he knew was that there was something about this boy he liked.

Then one day, Pop saw the boy in a fist fight. When the man saw that boy fight with his two little fists punching away as though they had a mission in life, little ripples ran up and down his spine.

Pop went home with the boy that evening. They talked of a brave and glorious future. The kid's name, of course, was Jimmy McLarnin. The McLarnin family was a large one and Jimmy's folks knew that Pop Foster was a good man to take care of little Jimmy. Pop and the boy tied up. Pop sold his fishing boats and left Vancouver with his two-fisted, baby-faced protégé.

Pop and the scrawny underfed kid lived in San Francisco for a while. Pop, who was a holdover from the bare-knuckle days, shaped the little fellow with the patient skillful hands of a sculptor. He taught Jimmy McLarnin every trick of attack and defense. When he thought that his boy was ready, Pop Foster started trudging around begging for a chance for his Jimmy to fight.

These two struggled right to the very top. Baby-faced Jimmy McLarnin became the "killer of the ring," one of the best fight attractions in the country. In 1933 he became the welterweight champion of the world.

For thirteen years, Jimmy McLarnin and Pop Foster travelled the fistic road, a pair of hard-bitten wanderers in quest of ring glory and gold. Always there was Pop to protect his Jimmy, standing outside the ropes and watching his boy fight, watching him with something glorious brimming up in his hard old eyes. Around the fight circuit they hated old Pop. They called him a grasping old man, a cauliflower ghoul who always drove a hard sharp bargain. But the old pirate always made sure that his Jimmy would get the best break.

Year after year they went along together in this way, shoulder to shoulder. Jimmy, the baby-faced killer could no more leave Pop than he could tear out his soul. Together they stood until Jimmy McLarnin retired from the ring and hung up his gloves forever. When he did that, though, he and Pop had made a fortune of $700,000 out of the prize ring. It was a partnership that really paid off.

YEARS AGO, OUT IN FARGO, NORTH DAKOTA, A CHAP NAMED Jack Hurley ran a boxing column that appeared in a string of newspapers in the prairie country. On the side he dabbled in the sport, managing a few small-time local fighters.

One day Hurley met a broken-nosed, tough-looking lightweight by the name of Billy Petrolle. The fighter needed money and hoped to earn a few bucks in the ring. Jack Hurley looked the unknown over and decided that maybe he could do something with him. He took Billy under his wing and became his manager.

Putting his typewriter on the shelf, Jack Hurley and his new fighter headed for New York and the big time. In every town along the way, Hurley sang the praises of his latest acquisition. "Watch that boy of mine," he would say. "Someday he'll make fistic history, mark my word. We'll make a lot of dough, yes, sir."

But Billy Petrolle was no ball of fire. He won a few fights but dropped many others. Still Jack Hurley kept his faith in Billy Petrolle as a great fighter. Hurley, a slim, quiet, intelligent fellow, and Billy Petrolle, broken-nosed, tough-looking, dressed in plain clothes and a cap, made an oddly assorted pair. They were inseparable and soon became a familiar sight wherever they went.

Then one day, Billy Petrolle decided that he had accumulated enough money to get along without fighting. He decided to quit the ring. He had earned the munificent sum of thirty thousand dollars, a small fortune.

Hurley agreed, and Billy Petrolle went home, married, and slipped back into obscurity. Jack Hurley, in turn, went back to pounding his typewriter and getting out his boxing column. When the pair returned to the prairie country, nobody missed them.

After about a year, Billy Petrolle came to Hurley with a problem and a proposition.

"Look, Jack," said the fighter, "I just got to fight, and that's all there is to it. This quiet life is all right, but I can't take it any more! What do you say, we try it again? Maybe this time I'll make a better fighter and we'll make a little more dough for ourselves."

"Okay," answered the willing Hurley, "I'm game to try again if you are. Maybe this time we will click."

Once again, Jack Hurley set out with Billy Petrolle for another crack at fame and the pot of gold. Neither of them considered the odds against them. And neither of them knew what was in store for them.

A sort of miracle took place for Jack Hurley and Billy Petrolle. The mediocre lightweight suddenly seemed to have found the fountain of youth! In no time at all, he became the most dangerous lightweight in the ring. He fought great fights against Jimmy McLarnin, Tony Canzoneri, and a flock of others. The hard hitters, the tough ones, the fancy Dans—Billy Petrolle met them all. Before he was through the Fargo Express, as Billy came to be called, was one of the greatest lightweights that ever lived. Nobody who saw Billy come into the ring wrapped in his familiar old Navajo blanket will ever forget him.

After a few years of spectacular activity, Billy began to slow up, and his manager, Jack Hurley, convinced him that he ought to retire. Reluctantly, the Fargo Express agreed. Still, by the time the comeback had come to its glorious end, Billy Petrolle, the washed-up, mediocre has-been, had not only become one of the great lightweights of history, but had earned the "little dough" he had come back to the ring to earn. Only, the "little dough" amounted to no less a sum than a quarter of a million dollars!

AMONG THE GOLD-HUNGRY PROSPECTORS WHO MADE THE mad rush to the frozen Yukon was a sixteen-year-old who thought he could make a few easy dollars as a prize fighter. He wasn't too successful. One day, a friendly mining engineer named Herbert Hoover told him that he was too intelligent to try to earn a living by having his brains beaten out. It might be a better idea to put those brains to the use for which they were intended.

Young Jack Kearns took the mining engineer's advice and began to seek the elusive buck in other ways. First, he quit the ring as a fighter. Then he returned to the States. He became a manager of a few mediocre prize fighters. Although he was strictly small time, Kearns was getting along, and his agile brain was constantly working for himself and his boys. It was just a question of time before smart Jack Kearns would hit the jackpot.

One day, he was sitting idly in a shabby dive when in walked a hobo. The hobo had not been in the place more than a couple of minutes when half-a-dozen tough characters picked a fight with him and tried to beat him up. At the first sign of trouble, the hobo went to work with his fists and Jack Kearns went to work with his brains.

The hobo turned out to be a two-fisted terror and wrecked the joint in the process of making the six hard characters wish they hadn't started in on him. When it was over and the casualties were being taken away from the field of battle, Jack Kearns climbed out from under the table and made for the tramp. In no time, the smart little manager had staked him to a meal.

That was how Jack Kearns found himself a new fighter to add to his stable. The two men formed a partnership composed of one set of agile brains and a pair of iron-hard fists and a physique to go with them.

Kearns began to get fights for his new charge. The ex-hobo won them quickly. The two men began to eat regularly, an art which had hitherto eluded them. The hobo thought he was doing fine. Jack Kearns was still figuring and calculating with that smart head of his.

There was no stopping the combination. Eventually Jack Kearns made the ex-hobo into the most famous heavyweight champion of all time. And with it, along the way, Kearns also managed the ex-hobo into a fortune of more than ten million dollars.

It is needless to point out that Jack Kearns' prize package was the immortal "Manassa Mauler," Jack Dempsey.

BOXING, MORE THAN ANY OTHER SPORT, IS CHOCK-FULL OF Cinderella yarns. Jim Braddock came off relief to win the heavyweight championship of the world, Jack Dempsey was once just a hobo riding the rods, and Joe Louis was a poor laborer before his fists began to carve out fistic history. But no fighter ever came from deeper obscurity and more abject poverty to achieve success than little Beau Jack.

Where he came from, no one knows, not even Beau Jack himself. As far as the sports world is concerned, his life began on the day a hungry and ragged little colored boy came trudging along a dusty road in Georgia. Tired and thirsty, the boy stopped at the caddy house of the Augusta Golf Club and begged for work.

For some odd reason, Bowman Milligan, Negro clubhouse attendant, took a liking to the ragged youngster. He found him a job at the club shining shoes.

It was more than a job that Bowman Milligan gave to Beau Jack. He gave him, as well, a home and friendship. He became for the boy the only parent he had ever known. A warm friendship grew up between the two.

One day the clubhouse attendant discovered an interesting thing about the ragged shoeshine boy. The kid could handle his fists and loved to fight. Young Beau took part in the battles royal that were staged at the golf club for the amusement of the members who liked to sit around in the cool of the evening over their drinks as half-a-dozen teenage youngsters belted each other around in a free-for-all. Beau Jack never lost a fight in those wild mix-ups.

It wasn't long before an idea occurred to Bowman Milligan. Why couldn't young Beau Jack go places as a professional fighter? He went to fifteen members of the Augusta Golf Club and made them a proposition. It was taken up enthusiastically. Each contributed fifty dollars to help finance Beau Jack in his new professional boxing career.

Under the tutelage of Bowman Milligan, Beau Jack took his first steps in the professional ring. At first he was no ball of fire. But whether he won or lost, Jack was a consistent crowd pleaser. They liked the slam-bang hurricane style he had acquired almost naturally. Soon it began to pay off. Beau Jack began to win consistently. There came a point when he had won twenty consecutive contests. On that day, Bowman Milligan had a serious talk with his protégé.

"Beau," he said, "I'm figuring you are ready for the big time now. We're going to New York. This is your chance, son, to make something of yourself and get some of the things out of life you deserve. I've done all I could. I gave you a job and a home and my friendship. Now you can get everything else you want with your own two fists."

What followed is history. Beau Jack moved into the big time, won eleven straight and went scooting into the headlines. Soon after Beau Jack crowned his glorious career with the most coveted title in fistiana next to the heavyweight bauble, that of lightweight championship. Thus it was that a simple colored boy out of nowhere paid off a man's kindness and friendship by living a truly Cinderella story of the ring.

IN ONE OF THE MOST THRILLING FIGHTS EVER SEEN IN MADI-son Square Garden, Henry Armstrong was knocked out by Fritzie Zivic in the twelfth round of a bout for the welter-weight championship of the world. The contest which took place back in 1941 was a memorable one but the mere record of the fight does not tell everything of a drama that never got into the headlines.

When Henry Armstrong started his journey up the road towards boxing fame, he was only a hungry, lonely and friendless little Negro. He was friendless, that is, except for Harry Armstrong, whose name he took and whom he called brother.

Along the road somewhere, a road that took Hammering Henry from the dusty back streets of St. Louis to San Francisco to Mexico City to New York, London and Paris, he acquired another friend, a roly-poly man by the name of Eddie Mead.

Mead became Armstrong's manager and the two trav-elled together by high road and low road. At every fight, Mead was in Henry's corner, watching him, advising him, fathering him. The partnership was more than just a manager-fighter combination. They were inseparable friends and each one of them thrilled to the other's joys and ached to the other's sorrows.

It was Eddie Mead who was in Armstrong's corner when the wonderful little fighter won the featherweight, light-weight and welterweight titles, honors that he held si-multaneously in a career that will never be matched by any fighter.

And it was Eddie Mead who sat and suffered in Henry's corner when Zivic took the welterweight crown from his boy. Mead got after Armstrong then and begged him to quit the ring for good. But game little Henry still had one ambition in life, to regain his lost crown before saying goodbye forever to the sport.

It was with great reluctance that Eddie Mead agreed to that last fight. With his usual keenness, he watched over Armstrong as he trained for the match.

On the night of the fight, Eddie Mead was not in his fighter's corner. He had suffered a serious heart attack. The whole fight mob knew that Eddie had a bum ticker. And nothing Eddie said could talk the doctors into letting him be present. They wouldn't even let him listen to the broadcast on the radio.

The fight, of course, went on without Eddie Mead. It saw a grand little champion reach the end of the road in a thrilling exhibition of heart and courage. With fifty-two seconds of the twelfth round gone, and with courageous little Henry Armstrong out on his feet, his eyes bleeding, his face a crimson mask, the referee stopped the butchery and gave the victory to Zivic.

Armstrong headed for his dressing room, threw on his clothes as quickly as he could, and rushed off to have his wounds treated. At the doctor's office, waiting for his boy, was his friend and manager, Eddie Mead, himself under the care of the same physician.

Armstrong looked down at his friend through swollen eyes. "I'm sorry I lost, Eddie," he said quietly.

Eddie Mead looked up at his fighter's cut face, his torn mouth and nose. Then he reached out and grabbed Henry's hand. "Go home, Henry," sobbed Eddie, "go home, you'll never fight again! Promise me you won't!"

Armstrong nodded slowly. "I'll never fight again," he whispered. "And I'll never forget you, Eddie!"

They sat there for many hours, the fighter and his manager, talking of the grand days of the past, the early and lowly beginnings, the three championships that had been held simultaneously. The roly-poly little man wept and let the tears run unheeded down his cheeks; the little fighter forgot his bruises and scars.

In the streets the fight fans were already beginning to read the details of the terrific battle that had taken place a few hours before in the Garden. Nothing was written about the scene that was even then being played out in a doctor's office between a sick and weeping manager and a beaten but not dishonored fighter.

ONE NIGHT, NOT LONG AGO, AT THE START OF THE SEVENTH round of a prize fight being staged in Washington, D. C., the referee walked over to a corner where sat a tired old man, his face a bloody mask. He shouted above the din of the crowd, "Do you want to come out?"

The beer-barreled fighter grimaced in pain and mumbled his answer through broken, bloody lips. "No! No!"

So ended the dizziest ring career in fistiana. So also came to an end a story of blood and slaughter, a tale of terror and comedy, bluster and ballyhoo. It was the dismal end of Tony Galento.

If a script writer had tried to palm off the story of Tony Galento as fiction, he would have been run out of Hollywood. But Tony Galento, the fighter, was real, as real as a little man named Joe Jacobs could make him by ballyhoo and imagination.

At best, Galento was never much of a fighter. In the ring, he was a grotesque puppet, a hairy human ox immune to pain, with a body padded with such thick layers of fat as to render him impervious to the hardest blows. He fought without grace and without science, grimacing and snorting through his broken nose as he wildly swung his short thick arms at his opponent, hoping to land but a single blow. If he did hit a man, down he went, and that man wouldn't get up in a hurry. Clumsy clown that he was, Tony Galento always had an authentic contempt for his adversaries. His popular ring slogan for victory will never be forgotten: "I'll moider de bum!"

Galento was everything an athlete shouldn't be. Beginning as an ice man, Tony continued as a home brew salesman, bartender, bouncer, and finally, owner of his own saloon. He always ate what he pleased, smoked continuously, drank. Never a paragon of politeness, he swaggered, bellowed and blustered. It is not too far-fetched to call him a throwback to the old saloon era of boxing. All he wanted to do was fight, be it fair or foul, in the ring or out.

Tony Galento was strictly a small timer on the down grade until he hooked up with that wily and tricky little manager, Joe Jacobs. Jacobs took that beer-guzzling, rough-and-tumble mug and began to build up a story around him. He began to whisper into Tony's ear that he was a great fighter, the best in the world. At the same time, Jacobs let the world know what a great fighter Galento was. Tony began to believe the story himself.

The fight fans began by laughing at the pretensions of the has-been fatso. Little Joe Jacobs kept the ballyhoo mills grinding on. He matched Tony with a couple of pugs. Galento wheezed to victory over them. Jacobs' claims got louder and louder. His fighter was now the best in the world. Not only that, he was entitled to a shot at the heavyweight title—against the great Joe Louis himself!

By clever and shrewd maneuver Joe Jacobs steered Two-Ton Tony, the clown, into a fight for the title. And the match took place on a night in June, 1939.

That night, incredibly, Tony Galento, that animated lump of lard, achieved a moment of greatness as a fighter. As the bell rang for the opening of the fight, Joe Louis, invincible champion of the heavyweights, shuffled out to the center of the ring. Tony Galento waddled out to meet him. The clown stooped in a crouch as the champion loomed over him, then suddenly lunged out with his ponderous fist in a left hook. The great champion, stunned momentarily, went groggily bouncing into a corner, practically out on his feet. The vast crowd rose to its feet, a single cry of shock on its lips. Tony Galento had the championship of the world in the palm of his ham-like hand. All that he needed to make the miracle come true was to hit the dazed champion another blow like the first one.

But the fat clown of the ring hesitated. He was accustomed to belting out bums, and he expected them to flop into the resin when he hit them. But this was the champion and Tony could not believe that he hurt him. So he stood in the center of the ring and waited, watching champion Joe Louis with his small suspicious eyes.

And that moment of glory which had almost made him a champion of the world, an immortal of the prize ring, slipped away from Tony Galento forever. The round ended and Louis recovered. Then Joe went to work on Tony, the clown who had dared to humiliate him. In the second round, the Brown Bomber gave the fat buffoon as murderous a beating as any fighter has ever absorbed. With cold fury and deadly precision, he destroyed the clown as a fighter. Tony, his face a red and bloody blob, refused to quit. He gave an exhibition of gameness rarely seen. Towards the end of the round, the champion dropped him for a count, but still Tony refused to quit. With painful slowness, the clown dragged his fat and unwilling body off the floor. As Joe Louis came at him again, Tony struck out blindly again and down went the champion for the second time.

It was Tony's last bid for ring glory. In the next round, his grotesque body could stand the punishment no longer. Helpless, bloody, Tony Galento went down to defeat. His bid for the heavyweight championship had come to an end.

Tony Galento came out of the ring cursing through lacerated lips: at the referee for stopping the fight; at his manager and seconds for not letting him fight in his own rough-and-tumble way. And his little manager, Joe Jacobs, screamed with him, insisting that the next time his fighter, Galento, would beat the great Joe Louis and take the title.

To prove his contention, Galento met Lou Nova in the ring three months later and gave that young fighter so cruel a beating that he had to stay in a hospital for months. Galento was on his way back to the top—and then came the blow. Wise little Joe Jacobs died. The Svengali-Trilby combination of fistiana was broken. On the day they buried the mortal remains of Joe Jacobs, Tony stood near the edge of the grave and held out his two fists before his face as the tears streamed from his eyes. "Joe, Joe," he sobbed, "what am I gonna do with these two fists now? Joe, they're no good to me any more!"

Tony was dead right. His fists were never good to him any longer. With the passing of Joe Jacobs, the incredible fistic career of Two-Ton Tony Galento really came to an end. He never again won a fight!

CROSS AND DOUBLE CROSS

You may recall Jackie Kid Berg, a young man who was quite a fighter back in the thirties. He was a lightweight from the Whitechapel district of London. His whirlwind style, blazing fists, and courage in the ring made him a standout in his day.

From the beginning of his career in the United States Jackie ran up a sensational winning streak against the best lightweights and welterweights in the business. Through all his fights, Berg was trained by clever, able Ray Arcel, the top man at his trade.

Now, Arcel loved a good fighter, and Jackie Kid Berg was every inch a fighting man. There was only one thing in Berg that Arcel did not particularly like. He was often needlessly cruel in the ring.

While he was training for his second fight against the unforgettable Tony Canzoneri, Ray Arcel brought a nice, clean-looking young man over to Jackie and introduced him to the famous fighter. As the stranger shook hands with Berg, he timidly said, "I was just wondering if I could have the honor of boxing a round or so with a famous fighter like you."

Jackie Kid Berg agreed willingly. As the stranger drew on his gloves, he turned to the Whitechapel slugger and said, "Please don't hurt me too much. I'm not much of a boxer, you know. I'm just learning the game and I like to box just for the sport of it, that's all."

However, when the two men squared off, Berg sailed into the young man and plastered the daylights out of him.
At the end of the round, with his face streaming blood from
many cuts, the stranger reproached Jackie for having given
him so severe a beating.

Jackie laughed. "My dear fellow," he said airily, "it's
against all the rules and regulations of boxing to pull your
punches. Ethics of the profession, you know!"

The years went by. Jackie Kid Berg shot up to the skies
and then began to skid. Eight years after he had given a
stranger a lesson in ethics, he was still at the game, a hard-
ened veteran whose best days were far behind him. He
took a fight with a tough young fellow named Johnny
McHale and came out of the fight with two badly bruised
fists. Berg had another fight scheduled for two weeks later
against some palooka from New Jersey. He didn't bother
to train, nor did he do anything about taking care of his
damaged hands.

On the afternoon of the fight, Jackie's fists were still
swollen and in horrible shape. The slightest touch was
painful. His handlers advised him to call off the bout, but
the Englishman needed the money badly. Finally, an hour
or so before fight time, Jackie was taken to a doctor to get
a shot of Novocain.

As the fight began, Berg faced the unknown palooka,
while at ringside sat the doctor who had fixed him up.
With the first exchange of blows, Berg realized that something was wrong. The shot had not been effective. Every
time he hit his opponent, a terrific pain shot up his arms.

Jackie Kid Berg took a merciless beating in that fight.
The unknown smacked him all over the ring. And, at ringside, the doctor chuckled and had himself a grand time.

At the end of the scrap, Berg crawled out of the ring,
walked over to the doctor and stuck his battered face into
that of the medico. "Say, doc," he muttered through gashed

lips, "I thought you said you were going to fix me up. What in the bloomin' 'ell did you shoot into my fists—water?"

"That's right!" said the doctor. "I gave you an injection of water, nothing else! You see, my fine friend, it's against all the rules to inject drugs into a fighter's hands. Ethics of the profession, you know."

The last words rang a familiar bell for Jackie Berg. He peered closer into the face of the doctor and then recalled where he had seen it before. It was the same man who had, eight years before, come to him in a gym asking for the honor of putting on the gloves with him for a bit of sparring. It was the same man whom he had so cruelly beaten up.

OLD SAM LANGFORD WAS ONE OF THE HARDEST HITTING heavyweights in the business. The "Boston Tar Baby" had just as much respect for his own punch as the next man, too. The first time he signed to fight in England, he showed up before the bout at the National Sporting Club in London. The promoter began to discuss the coming engagement with Belting Sambo. Among other things he told Sam that he could have his choice of any of three referees.

Langford shrugged his powerful shoulders and broke into a wide grin. "Uh-uh," he said. "That won't be necessary. I carry my own referee."

The English promoter threw up his hands in horror. "I'm sorry, Langford," he stammered. "We can't permit that."

Old Sam raised his ponderous arm and doubled his ham-like fist under the promoter's nose. "Boss," he said, "this is my referee!"

And it was. Langford knocked out his opponent in jig time that night. But there was another occasion when his "referee" failed him.

In 1911, Langford was matched with Bill Lang. Before the fight, Langford was approached with a proposition, namely, to throw the fight. Sam refused. He was too confident of achieving an easy victory over his opponent.

The first thing that seemed odd to Sam Langford as he sat in his corner was the gloves he was given to wear. A box containing the two pairs of gloves had been tossed into the ring. When the box was opened, Langford was astonished to see that the gloves were white. He saw immediately that the gloves had been ordered by Lang's manager purposely because white gloves would show up better against his own dark body and might therefore sway the judge's decision.

Sam shrugged it off, however. As far as he was concerned, he could win the fight under any conditions, white gloves or green or sky blue pink.

In the second round of the fight, Langford dropped the Englishman a couple of times. Sam grinned even more widely. He knew now for sure that he had an easy job on his hands. In the third round he again put Lang down for a short count. When he returned to his corner his manager berated him gently for not finishing the Englishman off for good. Langford promised to clean up the business in the very next round.

In those days, when Sam Langford really wanted to kayo a man, all he had to do was land five good punches, then turn his back and walk to his corner while they counted the poor unfortunate out. The trick usually worked. Well, on this occasion, old Sam wound up and let go with five terrific punches. Down went the champion of all Ireland and England. But, instead of being counted out as Langford expected, Bill Lang got up fairly fresh at the count of nine.

It was at this point that Sam Langford began to smell a rat. Through the fifth and sixth rounds, Lang kept going down and bouncing up again. As wobbly as he was, Lang still managed to stagger around the ring under Sam's hammering fists. And then, as Sam let loose a terrific hay-maker, Lang wavered out of the way and Langford missed. So strong was Sam's follow-through on the attempted punch that he went sprawling on his hands and knees on the mat. Before he could get up Bill Lang tapped the big Negro on the top of the head. Immediately, referee Eugene Corri stopped the bout, awarding the fight to Langford on a foul. There was many a sigh of relief from the sporting gentry around the ring who had made over-enthusiastic bets on the Englishman to win and who had now saved their wagers by the nature of the decision.

Old Sam refused to give up his gloves at the end of the bout. He insisted on taking them to his dressing room for the purpose of finding out why they had caused him to lose his vaunted knockout punch. He cut them open and learned the truth. Someone had deliberately stuffed his gloves with rabbit fur which was so soft and pliable that all the sting had been taken out of his blows! Imagine trying to knock out a man with a fistful of air!

SOON AFTER THE CRAFTY JACK KEARNS HOOKED UP WITH his new heavyweight, Jack Dempsey, the two men made a tour of the Southwest, meeting all comers. Kearns billed the young heavyweight as "The Next World's Heavyweight Champion" and made as sure as he could that nothing would happen to destroy the fine property he was handling.

Working with Kearns at the time was another foxy fel-low by the name of Bill McCarney, who knew his fistic onions and all the tricks in the fight game. With a pros-pective champion on their hands, the two astute gentle-men took every precaution to see that nothing unusual or untoward befell their juicy meal ticket. To make sure of this, Bill McCarney was sent ahead of the troupe for the purpose of digging up proper opponents in the towns they were to visit.

Dempsey was booked to appear in a certain Oklahoma hamlet and McCarney arrived there before the others. He had a terrible time trying to get a man willing to take on the terror of the ring. Finally, after searching high and low, McCarney managed to dig up a chap who didn't look as though the first breath of wind would blow him apart.

On the night of the fight, McCarney hustled to Kearns. "Look, Jack," he said hurriedly. "Dempsey better not waste too much time with this fellow. He's scared stiff and he's white as a sheet. Dempsey better pop him over before the natives get wise to the phony and lynch us!"

Kearns immediately leaned over the scowling Dempsey and whispered quickly in his ear. "Soon as that bell rings, Jack, I want you to tear out and get rid of this bozo in a hurry."

At this moment, Dempsey's opponent climbed into the ring and stripped off his bathrobe. Instead of seeing a man as white as a ghost in a sheet, Kearns was horrified to see a fine-looking chap whose skin was as red and healthy as that of an Indian. "Something's wrong," muttered the crafty manager. "Didn't McCarney say this guy was pale? I wonder if we've been double-crossed and this guy is a ringer! I don't like the set-up one little bit." And again he leaned over his fighter. "Jack," he whispered, "I think this guy is a ringer. Better take no chances!"

"What's the difference to me who he is?" growled Dempsey. "I'll stiffen him anyhow!"

The bell clanged and Dempsey, as savage a man as any man who ever lived, tore across the ring, threw a vicious left hook to the body, a right cross to the chin, and stepped back to let the red man sink to the canvas in a lifeless heap. The referee could have counted to a thousand forwards and backwards as far as the unfortunate fellow was concerned.

Back in their dressing room, Kearns muttered and growled as Dempsey started for his shower. Suddenly McCarney rushed in, panting for breath. "Whew!" he exclaimed. "Am I glad that's over! Come on, you two, let's get out of town fast!"

Kearns swung on McCarney and grabbed him by the coat lapel. "Listen, you dog!" he cried. "What did you try to pull on us tonight? What was the idea of switching opponents?"

"You're crazy, Doc!" retorted McCarney. "I didn't do anything of the kind!"

"Oh, yeah?" sneered Kearns. "I thought you told me the other guy was as white as a sheet?"

"And he was!" roared McCarney. "And he kept getting whiter and whiter all the time in his dressing room. It got so's I was afraid to put him in the ring the way he looked. So I got hold of a sponge and a big bottle of Mercurochrome and painted the sucker red from head to foot!"

Kearns threw back his head and howled. "How will the poor guy get that stuff off?" he asked.

McCarney shrugged. "That's his problem," he said. "My problem was getting it on!"

WHEN IRISH EYES ARE SMILING

Years ago, Mike McTigue was one of America's greatest fighters. "Bold Michael" they nicknamed him and he was as fancy a Dan as ever stepped in a roped arena. Mike fought them all, from middleweights to heavyweights. But he had one dream—to win the light-heavyweight championship of 'the world. In 1922, Bold Michael found favor with Dame Fortune for he was offered a fight in England against Georges Carpentier for the world light-heavyweight championship and $15,000 to boot. Mike McTigue quickly packed and left these shores. At last his big chance had come. He had within his grasp a world's title and to make sure there would be no slip-up, he began to train as soon as he got on the boat.

One morning when the ship was a few days at sea, the captain came to McTigue with a cable in hand and said: "Sorry, McTigue, 'tis bad new I have for you. You can stop your running and training. D'ja hear about the Senegalese?"

McTigue looked puzzled and replied: "Who's he—and why bother me with him—I'm busy training for my title fight with Carpentier."

The captain shook his head and said: "There isn't going to be a fight for the title. Last night Battling Siki knocked out Carpentier—just got the news by wireless."

So there was McTigue with no fight, once again frustrated in his quest for the title. The boat stopped in Queenstown, so McTigue, being a good Irishman, got off to tread the Ould Sod once again. Here, he found plenty of trouble he hadn't looked for because the Black and Tan conflict raged in all its fury and travel was difficult. However, he managed to motor down to Limerick only to find the Shannon between him and his native County Clare. Finally he found a man who would set him across for ten shillings but when McTigue got to the river, he saw that all he had was a little rowboat. Halfway across, a storm arose, the wind howled, the waves lashed and all but sank the rowboat, but Mike McTigue crossed the River Shannon—weary, worn-out and drenched to the skin. A few days later, he was approached by a Dr. George Devine, an Irish sportsman, who said: "Mike, how would you like to fight Siki—I'm going to Paris and may be able to arrange it?"

"Fine! Fine!" McTigue shouted happily, "I'll start training right away!" The very next day, he went out in the country to do some road work. But no sooner did he begin to run than a bullet whizzed by his ear. McTigue stopped, terrified. No one was in sight. Again he started to run and again a bullet whistled past his head. Poor Mike McTigue was plainly frightened to death! Suddenly, he saw a British Tommy appear from behind a tree, with his rifle cocked for action. "What are you shootin' at me for?" screamed Mike McTigue. "I'm only doin' a little road work!"

The soldier looked at McTigue and gruffly barked: "I've got orders to shoot anyone who runs!" So that was the end of Mike's road work.

In about ten days, McTigue heard from Dr. Devine who ordered McTigue to renew training for a Siki battle. But McTigue refused to start road work in Dublin for he had no desire to be mistaken for a clay pigeon by trigger-nervous British Tommies.

Since Battling Siki was unable to come into England, it

was decided to stage the fight on St. Patrick's Day, and, of all places, in Dublin. This famous meeting between Battling Siki and Mike McTigue was held in 1923. The arena was jammed to the rafters with a wild, shouting, frenzied mob of Irishmen. British Tommies patrolled the rooftops, covering the crowd with their guns. It was a bitter battle from the opening gong, and all through the fight, the wild crowd roared at McTigue: "Come on McTigue—nobody can lick an Irishman on St. Patrick's Day!" It goes without saying that McTigue won the decision.

THERE IS ANOTHER LITTLE STORY DEALING WITH A FIGHT fought on a St. Patrick's Day but this time the bout took place in the United States rather than Ireland. The immortal middleweight champion, Stanley Ketchel, stopped off at Cleveland one St. Patrick's Day to put on a show for the amusement of the local Irishmen. The feared Michigan Assassin offered one hundred dollars to anyone brave enough to go three rounds with him. According to the story, an unknown son of Erin, a musician named Ernest Ball, was desperately in need of the train fare to New York and agreed to enter the ring with the great Ketchel. Of course, young Ball took a severe lacing from the champion, but he did win the hundred dollars. With it, he got to New York where he eventually won fame and fortune as a song writer.

Ernest Ball wrote some of the most beautiful Irish songs that ever touched the heart of the world, but none is so well-known or so lovely as that one which glorifies St. Patrick's Day.

For the man who fought the great Stanley Ketchel to earn the money to start his career, wrote "When Irish Eyes Are Smiling."

PUBLIC BRAWLER

For many oldtimers there is only one heavyweight champion worthy of the title. That man was big, strong, fast Jim Jeffries. Those same oldtimers will tell you that the "Old Boilermaker" was the strongest and fastest heavyweight that ever pulled on a pair of padded mittens. In his prime, Jeffries could run the hundred with the best of sprinters. He had endurance as well, never tiring in the ring. Nor did punches ever bother the iron-jawed Jeffries. Once the hard-hitting Bob Fitzsimmons hit him flush on the point of the chin and Jeffries' head was not even tipped back by the force of the blow. As for the disappointed Fitzsimmons, he finished the fight with a fistful of broken knuckles.

Jim Jeffries had many thrilling, gory battles in his career but the fight that left him with bitter memories was the one he fought against a set-up named Jack Munroe. To his dying day, the Old Boilermaker regretted that fight, and for good reason as you will see.

After winning the title of heavyweight champion from Ruby Bob Fitzsimmons, Jeffries decided to cash in on his crown by boxing exhibitions all over the country. To bring out the crowds, he made the grand offer of one thousand dollars to any man who would step into the ring and stay four rounds with him. Jeffries went from town to town but no one turned up who was good enough to win the thousand.

However, Jim Jeffries arrived with his troupe in Butte, Montana, one unhappy night. As the famous champion stepped out on the stage before a packed house, his manager announced the usual offer of one thousand dollars to anyone who was bold enough to put on the gloves with big Jim and good enough to stay the distance.

Out of the audience stepped a big husky miner to accept the offer. His name, he said, was Jack Munroe. He was a miner from the Anaconda diggings and fancied himself as a fighter.

Having stripped to the waist for the encounter, Munroe stepped to the center of the ring to meet Jim Jeffries. There, in a whisper that could be heard in the last row of the theatre, Munroe said, "Jim, you better give me that thousand dollars right now, 'cause I'm aiming to lick you in them four rounds."

Jim Jeffries laid back his head and roared with laughter. Winking at his manager, he turned back to his corner determined to put the palooka in his place, but fast!

As Jeffries rushed to the middle of the ring to start the fight he ran into a terrific right hand punch from Munroe who brought his fist up from the floor to catch the surprised champion full in the face. Jeffries went down like a felled ox. He staggered to his feet before a count had been completed but Jack Munroe, the unknown fighter, not only managed to stay the route with the bemused champion but handed him a neat pasting as well. It was with a rueful face that Jeffries watched his unhappy manager count out the thousand dollars to the unknown miner before the view of the entire jeering and howling audience.

The result of the fight made Jack Munroe famous. Offers poured in from all over the country since everyone wanted to see the man who had licked Jim Jeffries in the ring.

Munroe made the most of his triumph. Wherever he went he strutted and boasted of what he could do to Jeffries in a return bout at the regulation championship distance.

Munroe got his wish faster than he expected. Jim Jeffries, still smarting from the knockdown he had suffered at the hands of this unknown, signed for a fight for the title.

It was the miner's big opportunity, but Jim Jeffries took no chances this time. He handed Jack Munroe a terrific beating, knocking him kicking in the second round. There was a lot of satisfaction for Jeffries but the lesson he had learned from their first fight was never forgotten. The rest of his boxing career, Jim Jeffries never again considered an opponent a set-up or a soft touch. And that was the only thousand he ever had to forfeit in an exhibition bout.

IT WAS A LUCKY LOT OF TOWNSPEOPLE WHO STOPPED TO watch a fight between a couple of kids, back in 1904. They saw a scrap that molded a man's character, a fight that none of them ever forgot with the passage of time. And if some of them murmured to each other, "That little fellow is bound to amount to something some day," they were right, as you will see.

The scene was a vacant lot in the town of Abilene, Kansas; the year was 1904. In those days, the tough cow-town tradition of Abilene was still a living thing for the boys of the community. Fights between them were usually fierce and rugged battles which often did not end until one of the contestants was stretched unconscious on the ground.

The town was split by the Union Pacific Railroad tracks. It was split in more ways than one, for the kids from the south side came from poor and humble homes, and those from the north side were rich. It was almost traditional that there be, at least once each year, a big fight between a south side and a north side boy. The fight was one of champions, if possible, since each opponent represented his own territory for everyone who lived in it.

No one remembers what trivial incident provoked this particular fight between the poor boy from the south side and burly young Wesley Merrifield, the rich man's son from the other side of the tracks. Certainly it couldn't have been planned that way, since Merrifield was a strapping husky youngster, big and heavy for his age, fast and strong, and his opponent, the poor boy, was slender for his 13 years, small and not too fast, not even good enough to play football with the neighborhood team.

No one had any illusions about how the fight would end. There seemed to be but one possible outcome. The bigger and stronger boy would win with ease. The only question was how long it would take.

Quite a crowd had gathered in the vacant lot to watch the contest. As expected, Wesley Merrifield pounded the kid from the wrong side of the tracks unmercifully. The poor boy's face was soon bruised and bleeding. Both eyes were blackened and swollen.

But the slender little fellow refused to quit. Despite his weariness and the punishment he was taking, he continued grimly.

The fight lasted a full hour. Towards its close, both boys were badly hurt. Both were bleeding and cut, and neither could lift his aching arms higher than his waist.

There was a moment's lull as the two glared at each other through half-closed eyes. The bigger boy fought for breath and finally managed to gasp, "I can't lick you. I'll quit if you will."

The other boy stuck out his chin. "I haven't licked you yet," he panted through swollen lips. "Come on, let's keep fighting."

Soon after, the fight was stopped with both near exhaustion. Whatever the result of the moment was, the little kid from the wrong side of the tracks was never picked on again.

The older and stronger of the two made quite a career for himself in the years to follow. When last heard of, he was superintendent of the famous St. John's Military Academy in Wisconsin.

The little fellow, overmatched for size but not for heart, also made his way up in the world. It was the steel will and the great heart of a champion that took the poor boy from obscure beginnings to the greatest task ever set a man —the leading of his country in a great war of extermination. For that poor boy from the wrong side of the tracks who did not know the word "quit" is none other than General Dwight D. "Ike" Eisenhower!

LITTLE RUNTS MAKE BIG STORIES

Nowadays the boxing commissions of the various states put all sorts of restrictions on fights that under-age youngsters are permitted to engage in. It wasn't always like that and no story of the ring is more to the point than Terry McGovern's.

Terry fought at the turn of the century. Some say that he started professionally when he was only a kid of sixteen. It is a fact that by the time McGovern was seventeen, he was already known as the "Terror of the Ring." "Terrible Terry" they nicknamed him, and the youngster richly deserved the name. He was the most savage and dynamic fighter of his time. He feared absolutely no one.

Before he was twenty-one years of age, Terry won the bantamweight championship of the world. That, in itself, is remarkable. Before he was twenty-one, he also won the featherweight title! Incredible, you say? That is not all for little Terry McGovern was so great a fighter, that before he was old enough to vote, he not only copped the bantam crown and the featherweight title but he also fought Frank Erne, the lightweight champion of the world—and knocked him out!

Indeed, Terry McGovern was a great little bruiser. He proudly strutted up and down the land with his titles and his hard swinging fists, winning all the boxing glory that there was for him to get.

And then, one day, in 1901, Terry came to Hartford,

Connecticut, to fight an unknown named Young Corbett, a lad from Denver, Colorado. The fight looked like an easy touch for unbeatable Terry.

He was sitting on the rubbing table in his dressing room, waiting for the call to go into the ring, when someone hammered on the door. A harsh voice on the other side growled, "Come on out of there, McGovern, you tramp, and take your licking."

It was Young Corbett. Little Terry McGovern, the greatest hitter and fighter of his weight in the fight game, turned white, not with fear but with rage. He sprang from the rubbing table. "Let's get out of here!" he shouted to his handlers. "Come on, I want to get at that guy!"

Trainer, manager, seconds instantly obeyed the Terrible Terry. Not one of them but thought that he would tear the challenger limb from limb.

But that night the boxing world was treated to one of its most shocking surprises. Before two rounds had passed by, the great, the invincible, the unbeatable Terrible Terry McGovern lay unconscious on the canvas, the victim of a knockout at the hands of the boastful little man from Denver. And above him, grinning down at his still form stood Young Corbett saying, "I told you you were a bum!"

That was the beginning of the end of the mighty atom of the ring. Terrible Terry McGovern never amounted to much after the beating he took at the hands of Young Corbett. And the surprising twist to the story is that, while McGovern won the bantamweight and featherweight championships of the world before he was twenty-one, and knocked out the lightweight champion of the world before he was twenty-one, he was also through and washed up as a fighter—before he was twenty-one!

THERE NEVER WAS A MORE AMAZING FIGHTER THAN THE pride of all England, the little Welshman, Jimmy Wilde! On a boxing tour of the British Isles, the incredible atom once fought 100 opponents in the space of 100 days—and beat 98 of them!

In his prime, Jimmy was a picture fighter. In spite of his weight—he never tipped the beam at more than 108 pounds—he could hit like a sledgehammer from his stand-up position.

Winning the flyweight championship from the famed Zulu Kid in 1911, Jimmy Wilde held the title for eleven long years during which he met and defeated men of all sizes and shapes, the tough ones and the fancy ones as well. In 1913 he won thirty-nine consecutive fights. Shortly after the first World War he defeated Pete Herman, the American who held the bantamweight title, in seventeen furious rounds that ended in a knockout of the heavier man.

Finally, in 1923, Jimmy Wilde, now a shell of his former self, came to the United States to display his fistic prowess. The mighty atom had put in a dozen gruelling years in the ring and was now past thirty. Meeting the sterling little Filipino warrior, Pancho Villa, Jimmy elected to mix it with the challenger and was knocked out in seven rounds. But, until he went down in defeat, Jimmy put on an exhibition of pure boxing form that was a revelation to the spectators. There never lived a fighter, be he flyweight or heavyweight, who could handle his mitts with more sheer grace than that grand little champion, Jimmy Wilde!

No LESS INTERESTING A FIGHTER THAN JIMMY WILDE WAS the lad who followed him as flyweight champion of the world, the little brown thunderbolt, Pancho Villa. The Filipinos have sent many fine young warriors to this land of ours in quest of gold and fistic glory, but none ever equalled the ability of the great little Pancho. He was a poor boy in Manila when he was first discovered and brought to this country by Frank Churchill, an old-time fight manager. In less time than it takes to tell, little Pancho rose from wretched poverty to riches, from a barefoot boy who roamed the Manila streets, to the flyweight championship of the world.

Pancho was one of the busiest and fastest hitters in the game. He was only a lad of nineteen when he was meeting the best men of his weight in fights of fifteen rounds or more. And it was in 1923 that Pancho Villa rose to international fame when he beat the great little Englishman, Jimmy Wilde, for the world's title.

Among the many fine qualities in the little fellow was his love for America, its institutions and its national holidays. It was a combination of that love and the fierce gameness in Pancho Villa's heart that sent him to an early grave.

Pancho was matched with Jimmy McLarnin for a fight that was to take place in Oakland, California, on July 4, 1925. Several days before the fight, Pancho developed a badly ulcerated tooth. When it was suggested that the fight be postponed, little Pancho refused. "It is an honor that I shall fight on July 4th before a crowd of Americans," he said proudly. "I will not disappoint them. I will fight on that day, and no other!"

True to his word, the little brown man was ready to go on that July 4th. The Jimmy McLarnin that he went into the ring to meet was the same smiling, baby-faced McLarnin who was later to become one of the greatest of our welterweight fighters. Pancho had to be at his best to cope with the pile-driving fists of his opponent. But, troubled by his ulcerated tooth, the little Filipino was below par.

And Jimmy McLarnin, already giving great promise of his future, was superb.

Little Pancho Villa took a terrific beating at the hands of McLarnin. The price he paid was high, far too high. A few days later, Pancho Villa died of gangrene caused by the ulcerated tooth, and aggravated by the severe punishment he had received.

He was only twenty-four years old when he passed away, and he was still the champion of his division with the best years of his life before him. In his own way, little Pancho Villa died for his adopted land, the land in which the little brown man considered it a great honor to fight on Independence Day.

DURING THE WINTER OF 1947, A NEW YORK-BOUND AIRLINER ran into trouble in a blinding snowstorm. Groping for an airport in southern New Jersey, it crashed into the tree tops in a densely wooded area, scattering its human cargo among the branches and snowdrifts.

The rescuers who hurried to the scene of the crash hastily bundled up the survivors and rushed them to a hospital in Millville for treatment. The casualty list was released. The usual investigation began.

An alert reporter checked the list of injured casually. The names meant nothing to him. Then he ran across an entry that seemed somehow familiar. it read: "William Papaleo, Hartford, Connecticut." He read it again. Then he rushed for the press wires. The flash was relayed to all sports pages in the land. William Papaleo was unfamiliar if you didn't know the name he used in the ring. But Willie Pep was a champion, the featherweight title-holder. That was different. And William Papaleo was Willie Pep, a fighter with one of the most glamorous records of the present era.

It was with considerable relief that fighting fans learned Willie's injuries consisted only of a broken leg and some minor bruises. A man could come back to the ring after such injuries. But when they found out that Pep's damage included several cracked veterbrae as well, the heads began to shake. Willie Pep was through.

But they didn't figure on Willie Pep himself. Had they stopped to think about this grand little fighter's past history they would not have given up on him so easily.

When Willie was a kid of fifteen, the burden of feeding his family fell squarely on his shoulders, for his father was incurably ill. All that little Willie could earn at the time was a measly nine dollars a week.

It didn't take the boy long to realize that he could not long continue to feed several mouths on that sum. He decided to earn a little more money fighting with his fists. Willie had won a number of bouts as an amateur even though he was so young, and had picked up a lot of brass-backed watches for his trouble. Now he turned pro.

The first purse of fifty dollars nearly floored young Willie Pep. He had never realized that there was so much money in the world. The unknown Hartford youngster fought on, winning bout after bout in sensational style. Hardly anyone outside his immediate circle gave him a tumble. Then, suddenly, the boxing world sat up and took notice. Young Willie Pep became a sensation overnight when word got around that he had won fifty-three consecutive fights.

No one knew, probably no one cared, that Willie Pep's sensational winning streak had been inspired by the fight he was making for his family. It was enough for the fans that here was a lad who had set up an amazing record. Maybe he really had something, they thought.

So they matched him with Chalky Wright for the feather-weight championship of the world. And little Willie Pep made it fifty-four straight victories and the world's championship, as well!

That was Willie Pep, the lad who became the youngest world's champion in boxing history at the age of twenty. And that was the Willie Pep that so many people were willing to give up on, when he was caught by fate in that terrible plane crash.

They brought the badly injured fighter back to Hartford. They covered his body with a plaster cast from head to foot. Everyone thought Willie Pep was through. Everybody, that is, but Willie himself and his faithful manager and handlers. They knew him too well.

The fans were already comparing Willie with the oldtimers like Terry McGovern and Abe Attell, when the whole sports world was electrified by the announcement that Willie was going back into action. Only five months after getting into that cast to hold his damaged back in place, Willie was slipping into the ring in Hartford on the road back to the top where he was sure he belonged. That was the first of a series of fights. His reflexes were bad, his timing was off, his hitting was feeble. But the next time out, Willie was a little better. And from then on the improvement was steady and rapid. Little by little, Willie Pep, with the same grim determination and drive that sent him into the ring as a boy, clawed his way right back to the spot he filled as the best featherweight fighting in the land!

They made Willie Pep the "Fighter of the Year" in 1945, and no one more richly deserved the honor. But, in my book, he's the fighter of this year or next year or any year you care to name!

IT WAS IN 1916, SHORTLY BEFORE THE UNITED STATES ENtered the first World War, that two Negro battlers crawled into the ring of the once-famous Broadway Athletic Club in a match that had attracted a great deal of interest. Both were well-known featherweights. The name of one was John Henry Johnson. The other was Walter Edgerton, better known as the "Kentucky Rosebud."

The Kentucky Rosebud had campaigned against the best in the world, and was credited with a knockout victory over peerless George Dixon, featherweight champion of the world. However, Johnson was a younger man and the rumors flew thick and fast that the Rosebud was on his way down the ladder after a long and creditable career. It was a battle between a man coming up and a man going down. Or was it?

On the night of the fight, the little Broadway Athletic Club was jammed to the rafters with a wildly excited crowd. Everyone present was eager to see how the younger and stronger Johnson would make out against the more experienced Kentucky Rosebud.

From the opening bell the men began to mix it fiercely. The fight was not only a matter of victory but there was also a question of prestige to settle between them.

The first round was even, so far as the spectators could determine. Each man gave and received terrific punishment. The second round was a replica of the first as the men stood toe to toe, neither giving an inch. In the third round, the Kentucky Rosebud brought the crowd to its feet as he sent in telling blows that had his younger and more vigorous opponent staggering around the ring. The crowd howled for the kill. As usual, the older man had won the favor of the sports fans through his ability, in spite of their doubts, to cope with Johnson.

The bell rang for the fourth round. John Henry Johnson, quick to revive from the punishment, came out dancing. Cocky and sure of himself, he was determined to regain mastery of the situation. His older opponent met him in the center of the ring, feinted once, and then caught him with a terrific blow to the chin. Johnson dropped to the canvas, then gamely struggled to his feet. The Kentucky Rosebud was ready for him. He danced in and shot over another left, then a right cross. Down went Johnson again. This time the referee counted ten over his prostrate form.

Again the Kentucky Rosebud had proved to skeptics that he could take the ring with anyone. Again he showed that he was still a leading featherweight no matter how much people thought he had slipped. Had he not just licked John Henry Johnson, one of the toughest little men around? That should teach any other young upstarts that there was still plenty of kick in the old boy!

Nothing unusual about the fight, you say? Well, there was plenty about the fight between John Henry Johnson and Walter Edgerton that was different. For example, John Henry Johnson, the young upstart, a mere boxing youth, was forty-five years old. The veteran, winner by a knockout in four rounds, Walter Edgerton, the Kentucky Rosebud, was on the night he fought, exactly sixty-three years of age!

STRANGE BEGINNINGS

Some of our great fighters have reached the top from strange and unusual beginnings, but none of them ever came to the ring from an odder background than John Gully, a heavyweight champion of the dim and distant past.

It was in a moment of generosity that Henry Pearce, heavyweight champion of the world in 1805, agreed to visit an English prison to box an exhibition bout for the entertainment of the convicts rotting away behind the dank and gloomy walls. On his arrival at the prison a frantic search was made to find some husky inmate to act as sparring partner for the champion. The toughest convicts wisely refused to toe the mark against the big bruiser who held the title. Finally, a victim was found in the shape of a man named John Gully who volunteered to step into the ring with Pearce. Gully, who had been an obscure butcher boy, was serving a long prison term.

The contest proved to be sensational. Not only did Gully hold his own with the champion, but he handed Pearce a severe beating before the bout was brought to a close. The news of the battle leaked out and spread far beyond the prison walls. A syndicate of prominent sportsmen used its influence to free John Gully from durance vile after exacting a promise from the former butcher boy that he would follow a career as a prize fighter if released. Hungry for freedom, Gully naturally consented to the bargain.

As soon as he was turned loose, John Gully took up the business of prize fighting. Before long he had won the heavyweight championship. The world was stirred. A man had emerged from behind the bars of an English prison to become heavyweight champion of the world!

Nor was this the end of John Gully's story. The ex-convict went on to create an even more amazing career for himself. After fighting for years without tasting defeat, John Gully retired. With the money earned in the ring, he bought a number of race horses. Two of his thoroughbreds won the English Derby, famous classic of Epsom Downs. John Gully became famous as a sportsman. Society took him up, royalty favored him. Soon pressure was brought on Gully to run for Parliament. He did so, and was duly elected. From butcher boy, to convict, to heavyweight champion, to Derby winner, to Member of Parliament! What a breath-taking career that was!

When John Gully finally died, all England mourned his passing. He left behind not only the story of an incredible rise from obscurity but also a fortune of two million dollars, an unbelievable record for a man who would not have given two cents for his own chances on the day Henry Pearce took it into his head to visit an English prison.

"COMING EVENTS CAST THEIR SHADOWS BEFORE" GOES THE line, but no one in that tough neighborhood in San Francisco thought much of the fight between a local kid and a rag-picker that took place on Brannon Street one day. The neighborhood kid was two-fisted little Eddie Hanlon, the terror of the town, avoided by man and boy alike. Everyone was sure that Eddie would grow up to be a first-class prize fighter. Eddie believed it too, and waited impatiently for the day he could step into the ring with gloves on.

The fact of the matter is that Eddie Hanlon did grow up to be a first-rate fighting man, one of the cleverest lads to pull on gloves. But this story takes place long before that, on a day when young Eddie and his cronies were playing baseball. No sooner had the game begun when a broken-down wagon, driven by another youngster Eddie's age, pulled up in the middle of the street. Eddie glared at the boy in the wagon who was busily sorting rags.

"Hey!" he barked. "Get that wagon away or I'll climb up there and bust you in the nose. G'wan, beat it!"

The young rag-picker gave Eddie a cold look and went on with his work. Eddie Hanlon reached up, yanked the driver off the wagon, and the battle was on.

The two boys fought for nearly an hour and the battle was fierce and bloody. Good as Eddie Hanlon already was, the young rag-picker, surprisingly enough, was more than a match for him. As a matter of fact, he handed young Hanlon a severe beating. It took half a dozen pitying neighbors to break up the fight.

Eddie wiped the blood from his battered face and looked with respect at his recent adversary. "Kid," he said at last, "you're some fighter. I thought I was tough but I got nothing on you. You sure can sling those fists! I'm going to go into the ring soon to be a pro and I'd sure hate to bump into you there! Say, did you ever think of professional fighting?"

"Yeah," replied the young rag-picker. "Every once in a while I stop to say to myself, why don't you make some real dough boxing? Maybe I will some day. And let me tell you, you're a pretty good scrapper yourself. I ain't anxious to run into you in the ring, either."

Well, the fates took the matter in hand. Eddie Hanlon and the young rag-picker did meet in the ring, not once but three times in all. In every case Hanlon found his opponent just as tough to handle as he had been the first time they met in a street fight. Three times the boys met, three times the rag-picker won! And while Hanlon became a fine fighter, clever and hard-hitting, it was the rag-picker who went on to greater glory. Ring history records him as one of the greatest of the little men of the ring. He held the featherweight championship of the world for ten long years. From rag-picker to riches went Abe Attell, and he can thank a street fight for starting it all.

LOOKING BACK THROUGH THE YEARS ONE CAN RECALL A parade of fistic giants who, by virtue of their size alone, should have become champions. Most, however, ended up as clumsy tragic clowns. Among them were such as Ray Impellitiere, touted as a fighter who might one day become champion, but who fell apart, in sections, every time someone hit him. Earlier, there was a European champion named Herr Plaacke who came to the States to try for the heavyweight crown, a little fellow standing a mere six feet, nine inches tall, and weighing 380 pounds or nearly one-quarter of a ton, the equivalent of two Joe Louis's in his prime. He was sent into the ring against 160-pound Kid McCoy and the poor giant was almost slaughtered. And, of course, there was Primo Carnera, the Sequals Gargoyle, homely, buck-toothed giant who was jobbed into the heavyweight title only to be massacred by the smaller Joe Louis.

But there was one exception to the rule, a cowboy from Kansas who stood six feet, seven inches and weighed 260 pounds. He had a terrific punch, probably the hardest of any owned by a big fellow. He was clumsy and awkward and not much of a boxer, but when he was in shape, he could take it till the cows came home and still have enough left to flatten his opponent if he got a good crack at him.

Strangely enough, the Kansas giant started in the ring

as a quitter. Jimmy Bronson, once a celebrated prize fight manager, the chap who later started Gene Tunney on the road to the heavyweight crown, tells the story of the clumsy giant who started his ring career in cowardly fashion.

Bronson, many years ago, owned a saloon in Joplin, Missouri. One day, this big cowboy came into the saloon and asked Bronson to manage him. Bronson, who knew fighters, laughed aloud. "I can't waste my time with a clumsy amateur like you. Why, man, you're twenty-six years old and you've never even worn a boxing glove! I've got a middleweight fighter half your size by the name of Jeff Clark who could beat you any day of the week."

"I'll fight him if you want me to," replied the giant. "Or anybody else you pick for me. I'm broke and I need the money."

"You can't fight my middleweight," answered Bronson with contempt, "but I'll get you a man closer to your size. Lick him first and then maybe I'll let my boy mess around with a guy like you."

The giant cowboy was matched against the oldtimer, Joe Cox, a mediocre light-heavyweight. Jimmy Bronson acted as referee. In the fifth round, Cox nailed the huge hopeful with a right to the chin. The giant seized Bronson in panic and held him between himself and Cox while maneuvering clumsily towards the ropes. As soon as he felt them at his back, he dropped Bronson and jumped clear out of the ring.

The giant was tearing off his gloves when referee Bronson leaned down towards him and screamed furiously, "You big lummox! You're nothing but a quitter! You're scared!"

The giant calmly tossed his gloves into the ring. Then he answered in his Kansas drawl, "Mr. Bronson, it's a smart man who knows when to quit. I'm no fool, and tonight's not my night!"

Jimmy Bronson's face turned red with rage. "No night will be your night!" he roared at the giant. "You'll never make good as a fighter. I wouldn't manage you for anything in the world. You'll always be a flop. You're a quitter!"

Well, that same clumsy giant who had never even worn a boxing glove till he was twenty-six, came along in 1915—when he was just twenty-nine—to knock out Jack Johnson in 26 rounds in Havana, Cuba. He won the heavyweight championship of the world and, in time, made himself a million dollars. The name of that giant who fooled so wise a man in boxing as Jimmy Bronson was Jess Willard!

DURING THE FIRST WORLD WAR, THE BATTLESHIP SOUTH Carolina had in its crew a husky, blustering, boastful sailor who was noted as a pop-off guy. This sailor knew nothing about the art of boxing but had been embroiled in a number of rough and tumble brawls because of his propensity for running off at the lip.

On one cruise, his ship was bound for Norway. The husky young sailor was sitting on a turret minding his own business, thinking of the fun he was going to have on shore leave when the vessel reached port at Oslo, when someone came up to him and snapped, "Chaplain wants to see you in the athletic office."

Surprised, the husky sailor went below. The chaplain quickly came to the point. He informed the sailor that he wanted him to substitute on the boxing program which he had arranged for the entertainment of the crew. The man supposed to meet a certain mess steward was ill and there was no one else to take his place.

At first, the husky sailor refused to go into the ring. He told the chaplain that he knew nothing about boxing and, what was more, he had heard that the mess steward in question was no man to play around with in a ring. However, when the chaplain gently reminded the husky sailor that if he refused to go through with the bout there might not be shore leave for him when the ship docked at Oslo, the young man quickly took the hint. He was willing to do anything not to lose his precious liberty.

The fight went exactly one round. The husky sailor connected with a wild swing, the mess steward went down and out for the count.

Although he didn't know it at the time, that fight started a new life for the sailor. To begin with, everyone began patting him on the back and telling him what a great fighter he was. This tickled the young fellow, and before he knew it, he was thinking seriously about becoming a prize fighter. When the war ended, he did enter the ring in quest of ring fame and glory. In time, he got to be quite a fighter, too. In fact, he became good enough, by 1932, to be recognized as the official heavyweight champion of the world. And the name of the fighter who became a pugilist only because he wanted his shore leave was Boston's Jack Sharkey.

ALONG BROADWAY THE NAME OF SAM HARRIS WILL EVER BE remembered when the roll call of great producers is taken, but even if he should be forgotten as a showman, his name will always be linked with the great fighter he once discovered in an obscure Brooklyn ring.

People in the theatre are frequently found around the sports scene, and Sam Harris was no exception. Early in his career, Harris took a crack at horse racing and at one time owned six thoroughbreds in which he had great faith. One day he entered four of his fastest horses in a single race in the hope that at least one of them would be a winner. When his horses finished in the last four places in the race, Harris traded all the animals for a prize fighter and began to look elsewhere for his sports thrills.

He spent all his earnings on the boy as he brought him along the road to the championship he was sure was his for the asking.

One night Harris matched his protégé with an unknown palooka from Brooklyn. Certain that his fighter would take the tough little Irish pug who was supposed to be a set-up, Harris was supremely confident. The unknown Irish kid from Brooklyn met him halfway. Sock! Bang! Down went Sam Harris' fighter, down and out! The Irish palooka had scored a knockout with the first punch.

Sam Harris was not at all disturbed or dismayed. He collared the victor as he left the ring. "Hey, kid," he shouted, "you've got a great punch. Who ever said you were a bum? What do you say you sign up with me?"

"Nothin' doin'," replied the Brooklyn boy. "I ain't hankerin' to be a fighter. Just wanna make a little dough, that's all."

"You're crazy, kid!" yelled Sam Harris. "I can make a champ out of you. Come on, let's sign a contract!"

The Brooklyn unknown refused but Sam Harris was stubborn. He haunted the kid for days and finally convinced him that he was destined to be a ring champion. Sam Harris signed him to a contract, while his friends laughed and said that the new kid would be no better than the old one.

Sam had only this to say. "That kid's a diamond in the rough. He'll be a great fighter. I'm going to manage him into a title!"

Sam Harris was as good as his boast. He did pilot the unknown from Brooklyn to a world's championship. Sam made a fortune with the boy.

The title the boy won was that of featherweight champion of the world. With his fiery little fists he punched out a million thrills for fans who would never have heard of him had it not been for Sam Harris. Who was that fighter? The one and only Terrible Terry McGovern, inch for inch, and pound for pound, the greatest fighter in the game!

LEW JENKINS DIDN'T HAVE A PICNIC ON THE ROAD TO FAME. In his youth, he knew poverty and loneliness. He picked cotton and he worked in a blacksmith shop. Early in his teens, Jenkins left home and joined that great army of depression kids who wandered from town to town looking for work. Perhaps it was the long hours under the burning Texas sun that made Lew Jenkins the skinny, raw-boned, vicious guy he was in the ring. Ten hours a day in the fields would make any hungry youngster a bit cruel.

When Jenkins was only eighteen, a friend told him that Jim Braddock, then champion of the world among the heavyweights, was scheduled to appear in an exhibition bout at nearby Dallas. Lew decided to see the champion perform. He had no money for carfare but that didn't stop him. He began to hike for the big town.

One afternoon, about two days before the exhibition, the promoter heard a loud knock on his door. "Come in!"

he growled. A skinny boy, dirty, worn, tired, entered the office. It was Lew Jenkins, the cotton field worker, dressed in dusty and patched overalls.

"What do you want, kid?" snapped the boxing promoter impatiently.

"Mister," drawled the kid, "ah want a fight. Anybody!"

The promoter sized up the frail-looking Jenkins and smiled. "Well, son," he said, "there is an opening on the card, but it's a tough boy and I can't pay much..."

"Never mind," interrupted Lew, "ah don't care what ah get paid, so long as ah kin fight!"

"Better get a little training," advised the promoter. "It's Moon Mullins you'll be meeting in the ring!"

"Okay," snapped Lew Jenkins, "I'll be there!"

Had Lew known anything about the boxing game, he would have realized that the Moon Mullins he was supposed to fight was a seasoned veteran, one of the best featherweights in the country at the time. But Jenkins did not know. What is more, he left that promoter's office with just a single dollar in his pockets to tide him over until the fight. For two days, he lived on that buck, eating oatmeal and milk and nothing else.

A huge crowd packed the arena on the night of the Braddock exhibition, and they saw one of the most stunning fistic attacks a fighter ever made when that skinny, unknown youngster crawled through the ropes to meet Moon Mullins in a preliminary match. The raw young kid smashed his way to a bloody victory against a seasoned and experienced foe, and made it look easy. The whole thing was hushed up quickly to save Mullins' reputation. It would be highly embarrassing to a leading featherweight if it ever became known that he had been licked by an unknown amateur.

When the fight was over, the promoter handed Lew Jenkins his reward for the evening's work. It amounted to the munificent sum of four dollars. Jenkins thanked the gentleman, and went back to the fields. Nothing more was heard of him for several years.

Then, when Lew Jenkins was an obscure blacksmith with a cavalry outfit of the regular Army, he began to engage in fights when on furlough. The little sideline brought him only coffee-and-cake money, but Lew wasn't thinking of anything else until—romance entered his life. Lew Jenkins met the beauteous Katie. It was then that the obscure small-time fighter took the step that led him to fame and fortune. Lew married the lovely Katie. After the wedding, she told him her greatest ambition. Katie wanted to see the big buildings in New York. Would Lew take her there?

Lew would. He bought a broken-down jalopy and drove Katie to the big city all the way from Texas. Lew didn't have a dime when the couple arrived in New York. Unknown as well as broke, Lew Jenkins went to a boxing promoter and begged for a fight. Luckily, and for the second time in his life, Lew found himself in the right spot when a substitute was needed. And he knocked out his man!

They matched him with another fighter and Lew won again by a knockout. The rags to riches saga was well on its way. The fight mob went wild over Lew Jenkins' murderous sock. Katie, the beautiful Katie, had barely seen the wonderful sights of New York when Lew Jenkins had won the lightweight championship of the world.

With fame and money, things began to happen to the new lightweight champion. No longer was he the hungry soldier who used to fight for chicken feed when on furlough. No longer was he living from hand to mouth, thankful when he found a place to lay his head after a tough scrap. He was riding high, wide and handsome. Nothing was too good for the champion!

Champ to chump is an old story in the fighting game. Lew Jenkins began to lose fights. He lost his title. He lost all his new-found friends, all his money, and finally, he lost his beautiful Katie.

So it was back to rags again for Lew Jenkins. He re-enlisted in the Army. Again, he began to fight when on furlough, as he used to do in the days before he became champ. But the old flame wasn't burning in Lew Jenkins any more. He took beatings. His saga was over. From rags to riches to rags again, the old story of many a fighting great, that's the sad tale of the skinny hard-hitting boy from Texas, Lew Jenkins.

SOME YEARS AGO, AN UNKNOWN YOUNGSTER CAME TO EDDIE Mead, and asked the fat man to manage him. The kid had been an amateur fighter, and had scored a small measure of success.

"I'm a good fighter," pleaded the youngster, "and some day I'll be a champion!"

Big, good-natured Eddie, always on the lookout for boxing greats, took the slight, dark-haired youngster under his wing and booked him for several bouts. Unfortunately, the boy proved a disappointment. He was a flashy kid, something of a dancing dude, but he just wasn't a great fighter. He lost more often than he won. In fact, he almost had his brains belted out in several fights.

Although Eddie advised him from time to time to quit the ring and find some other way to make his living, the kid persisted. He was determined to fight his way to fistic fame. "I'm letting you go," said Eddie. "I can't manage you any longer because I'm going to be too busy with another kid I just picked up. His contract cost me five thousand bucks and I think he'll be a champ for sure. Sorry, son. You're on your own now. Take my tip and quit the ring. You'll never be a good fighter!"

The boy turned white with anger. "So you don't want to manage me, huh?" he snarled. "Give me up for some unknown punk who probably isn't half the fighter I am, will you? You're nuts, Mister Mead! You'll regret this, because I am going to be a champ some day, and that new punk of yours will never get anywhere!"

"I don't blame you for being sore," answered kind-hearted Eddie Mead. "It's a fact my new kid is only a shoeshine boy I took off the breadline, but he's going places. And if you'll quit the ring, you'll go places, too!"

Time proved Eddie Mead right! The new fighter he had picked up became a great champion. Mead made a fortune while piloting him to three world's championships, all held simultaneously! That new fighter, for whom Eddie dropped his promising youngster was the featherweight, light-weight and welterweight champion of the world, Henry Armstrong!

As for the other boy whom Eddie dumped in favor of Hammerin' Henry, the manager proved to be correct. He never did become a great fighter, much less a champion. But he had taken Eddie Mead's advice to find a future in some other field. Today he is well known as the motion picture star, George Raft!

ON A NIGHT IN JUNE, MANY YEARS AGO, A BRITISH FREIGHTER dropped anchor in a small port of the French West African colony of Senegal. The captain, who was short-handed, sent a number of his biggest and roughest men ashore to pick up likely natives to fill out the crew.

Three of the toughest sailors from that freighter came across a lone Senegalese native who looked healthy enough to make a good seaman. They attacked the barefoot Senegalese on the spot, only to receive the surprise of their lives. In a short but desperate and bloody fight, the Senegalese with well-aimed and crushing blows of his fists stiffened all three of his attackers.

The young Negro, only recently out of the African jungle, was a fifteen-year-old boy named Louis Phal.

Hiding in a doorway near by, and watching the fight, was a Frenchman who happened to be a small-time manager of prize fighters. With an eye for an easy dollar, he lost no time in trying to convince young Louis Phal that his future and fortune lay in the ring. Easily persuaded, the Senegalese, unschooled and nearly savage, deserted the African jungle to become a member of the civilized world as a prize fighter. He took the ring name of Battling Siki.

Siki received his baptism of fire on a night in 1913, in the French city of Toulouse. No bigger than a middleweight, he fought an experienced and veteran French heavyweight. The youngster, barely sixteen years of age, won by a knockout after a brutal struggle.

Battling Siki fought again and again, always matched with bigger, stronger men who knew all the cruel tricks of their trade. Always he won. When hurt or stung, the young Senegalese was like a black jungle cat savagely striking out until his opponent lay unconscious at his feet.

The fame of the wild boy from the African jungle was growing rapidly when the first World War engulfed Europe. Battling Siki enlisted in the French Colonial Forces. After the war, a hero in the eyes of the civilized world, he returned to Paris, on his broad chest the Croix de Guerre and the Médaille Militaire.

Battling Siki went back to the ring, for he loved the savagery of the sport. He also loved pleasure. He never trained. Champagne, women, parties, all these filled Battling Siki's crowded days and nights. When he fought in the ring, this magnificently gifted fighter won consistently.

Finally, Battling Siki battled his way to a shot at the light-heavyweight championship of the world, a title held at the time by France's idol, Georges Carpentier, greatest heavyweight prize fighter in its history.

The match set all France afire. Fifty thousand Frenchmen came to see the battle, the largest fight crowd in Paris records.

The bout itself was memorable. It was not only one of the wildest, bloodiest, and most savage combats in the long history of fistiana, but also one of the foulest. Gorgeous Georges Carpentier, realizing that he had met his match in the former African jungle boy, tried every conceivable trick to win. On his side, Battling Siki was so enraged at the cruel tactics of his adversary that he reverted to the jungle too. Carpentier was in ghastly shape when the referee, to save the glamorous Frenchman from the ignominy of defeat by a knockout, stopped the fight in the sixth round and awarded the victory to him on a foul.

For a moment, the great audience sat stunned. Carpentier lay on the ring floor, his face beaten into a bloody pulp. Then pandemonium broke loose at the decision given by the biased referee. Seats were torn from their moorings and tossed into the ring. Angry thousands tried to storm forward from all parts of the arena as gendarmes rushed to the rescue.

During the commotion, the judges held a hasty consultation. Minutes after the fight ended, a new decision was rendered. It was "Winner by a knockout—Battling Siki!"

The cries of the mob changed to cheers. Battling Siki was lifted to willing shoulders and swept out of the arena, to be paraded up and down the streets of Paris.

Now the former barefoot native became the idol of all France. He played the role to the hilt. His wild antics, in and out of the ring, became the talk of the boulevards. He had only to appear in the streets or at the table of a favorite café to bring flocks of women to his side seeking his favor. And what pleased him most was to promenade the Grands Boulevards of Paris with a lion on a leash!

The pride and arrogance of the new light-heavyweight champion, the confidence he had in his skill and ability as a fighter are indicated by his agreement to meet one of America's best fighters, Mike McTigue. Not only did Siki agree to meet the Irishman in Ireland but he also agreed to the date proposed by Mike—St. Patrick's Day!

Siki defended his crown against McTigue in a Dublin arena jammed with frenzied Irishmen howling for his blood. Soldiers stood guard at ringside with fixed bayonets. Ireland, at the time, was in the throes of the black and tan "troubles."

As Battling Siki entered the ring, a giant explosion rocked the arena. A bomb had been set off near by. Despite the tenseness of the situation, Siki fought Mike McTigue twenty rounds to a decision. And, as everyone expected with an Irishman meeting a Negro in Dublin on St. Patrick's Day, the decision went to McTigue.

Shortly afterwards, Battling Siki came to America with the heavyweight title as his goal. But high living had taken its fateful toll of that magnificent black body. Siki won a few fights, lost a few fights. Before making his bid for the heavyweight crown, he tried to reclaim his lost light-heavyweight title. Paul Berlenbach, one of the hardest hitters in the ring, blasted Siki's fond hopes by knocking him cold. It was the beginning of the end. Battling Siki began to lose more and more often, and to live higher and higher.

Close to midnight, on December 15, 1925, some two years after Siki had arrived in the United States, a policeman walking his beat in New York's Hell's Kitchen stumbled over a body sprawled face down in a rain-soaked gutter. It was Battling Siki, two bullets lodged in his back.

The revolver which had fired the shots was on the sidewalk nearby.

The crime was perfectly executed. To this day, the murderer of Battling Siki has not been found. So far as everyone was concerned it was the end of the story for Battling Siki, age 28, the man from the African jungle who had sought fame and pleasure in a civilized world only to find death in a wet gutter far from his Senegal home.

THIRD MAN IN THE RING

Few people realize the importance of the referee in a championship fight. If he's doing his job properly no one either sees or hears him as he keeps a watchful eye on the fighters. But there have been times when the referee's actions have been more important than the skill and punch of his charges. In fact, it is known that the crown has changed hands because of a referee's slip.

There is, for example, the case of John L. Sullivan who might never have lost his heavyweight crown had not the referee permitted wily Jim Corbett to pull a cute trick before that memorable battle even started. As the referee called the fighters to the center of the ring to explain the rules, Gentleman Jim suddenly threw one arm around Sullivan's neck and, with the other, struck John L. a short but paralyzing blow under the heart. Then he turned innocently to the startled referee and asked, "Is that what you mean by punching in clinches?"

The referee could only nod his head in reply. Grinning to himself, Corbett went back to his corner, leaving the great Sullivan gnashing his teeth with rage and humiliation.

The surprise punch landed before the fight began helped lick the great John L. And it was because a referee permitted himself to be hoodwinked.

Then there was the time the heavyweight title changed hands with the challenger on the floor of the ring waiting for the referee to give him the nod. This happened one night back in 1930 when the German heavyweight challenger, Max Schmeling, fought Boston's Jack Sharkey for the title. In the fourth round, Schmeling went down from a punch he claimed was foul. Crowley awarded the fight to the German who was still sitting on the canvas.

On another occasion a referee lost a title for a great heavyweight fighter because he didn't count to ten fast enough. That was when Jack Dempsey, former champion, met Gene Tunney in their return engagement in Chicago. Dave Barry was the referee. When Dempsey knocked Tunney down in the seventh round and towered over the fallen champion ready for the kill, Dave Berry wasted five precious seconds trying to get Dempsey to move to a neutral corner. It is possible that had he begun the count when Tunney went down, Dempsey would have regained the heavyweight championship and become the first man in his division to do so.

But referees don't always pull boners. Sometimes they have courageous decisions to make and give them without hesitation. Take Jack Daugherty, for instance. Jack served as third man in the ring at the historic Jack Dempsey-Tommy Gibbons battle at Shelby, Montana, July 4, 1923. Shelby was a boom town, populated by many rough citizens who put up all their capital to pay Dempsey's purse. Tommy Gibbons fought for nothing. The angry citizenry of Shelby rooted hard for Gibbons to win the title from the man who had cleaned them out. Before the fight began, gunmen warned the referee, Daugherty, that he would be killed if he decided for the man who had bankrupted the town. When the fifteen rounds ended, referee Jack Daugherty, without a moment's hesitation, stepped forward and lifted Dempsey's right arm in token of victory. Then, without flinching, he walked out of the arena. Not a single hand was laid on him, not a single gun was flashed. A referee's courage had defied the wrath of a town gone broke and saved the crown for a champion.

SPEAKING OF REFEREES, THEY TOO HAVE THEIR ODD MO-ments in the ring. For fans who complain of partiality when their favorite drops a decision, this first little anec-dote ought to show them what real bias is. It happened in a fight between Kid McCoy and some unknown palooka whom the Kid agreed to take on for some easy money. In the very first round, the unknown closed his eyes and con-nected resoundingly with the Kid's jaw. Down went the great McCoy with a bang like a thunderclap. The referee, who was McCoy's man, just couldn't believe his eyes. He stood, mouth agape, staring at the fallen McCoy for a full minute before he began to count. Then he got down on his knees, put his lips against McCoy's ear, and began to bel-low the count as loud as he could roar, trying to rouse the Kid from his slumber. By the time the count reached five, the referee was out of breath and the Kid was still coma-tose. The referee stopped yelling and, leaning still closer to McCoy, took the fallen fighter's ear between his teeth and bit as hard as he could. He continued to chew and chew on the ear until it looked like raw hamburger, but still McCoy continued to count sheep.

The fans, as you can well imagine, were in an uproar at the goings on in the ring. Finally, despairing of ever get-ting McCoy to his feet, the referee got up, brushed off his trousers, shrugged helplessly, and shouted at the top of his voice, "Ten—and out!"

BACK IN THE DAYS OF THE FIRST WORLD WAR, YOUNG OTTO, who had been a famous fighter some years before that, became a referee. On one occasion, he was assigned to referee an entire card of fights. After handling all the preliminaries with neatness and despatch, Otto was told that the main event could not go on because one of the fighters had failed to show up. The crowd, bitterly disappointed, began to grow ugly. Young Otto stepped into the center of the ring and lifted his arms for silence. "Just a minute, folks," he said when the uproar subsided, "I'll get a substitute for the missing man. Just take it easy for a minute."

He left the ring, only to reappear a couple of minutes later dressed in tights and with gloves laced on. Clambering back through the ropes, he walked towards the empty corner and waved to the crowd. "I'm taking the place of the missing man myself!" he shouted.

His opponent, a dangerous lightweight, sprang from his corner. "Hey," he said, "you can't do that. You're an old man, and besides you're the referee. We can't fight without a referee."

"I don't need a referee," replied Young Otto with a smile. "Go on back to your corner and come out fighting at the bell. What's more, I'll count you out myself!"

The appropriate sequel is that Young Otto did flatten out his opponent in four rounds, counting the young man out himself and giving him a double count just to make sure he was being absolutely fair and honest about the whole thing.

NOBODY READS A RECORD BOOK FOR EXCITEMENT, BECAUSE statistics don't give you what lies behind the cold dry figures. There is, for example, a one-line entry in the long and glorious record of Terrible Terry McGovern, which reads: "Oscar Gardner, beaten by K.O. in four rounds." The date indicates that McGovern was at the height of his fame when he beat Gardner and a casual reader is satisfied that the fight went strictly according to schedule. But the record book leaves out something—the truth behind the one-line entry, and how a referee played his part in keeping the name of McGovern untarnished by defeat.

When Terrible Terry was bantamweight champion of the world, he was more than just a great little fighter. He was a savage little bundle of blazing energy. Often the little guy fought and licked featherweights and lightweights. He even took on welterweights and beat them easily. While Terry was riding high and wide another little fellow came along to challenge him. His name was Oscar Gardner.

Gardner, also known as the Omaha Kid, was a terrific puncher in his own right. He was as big a boaster as he was a hitter, but he happened to be a guy who could make his boasts good. After bowling over a number of men in the division, Gardner yelled for a match with the champion. Terrible Terry ignored the big mouth. The Omaha Kid was beside himself with rage at the champion's sneers.

"I can lick McGovern any time he's game enough to fight me," boasted the Omaha Kid. "And what's more, I'll knock him out. Go on and tell him what I said."

Finally, the match was made. Nobody thought Gardner would be able to stand up against the ferocious fists of the champion.

At the bell beginning the fight, Terrible Terry rushed out of his corner as though he was going to rip his opponent to pieces. When he reached the middle of the ring he found that the Omaha Kid had the same idea. The two men met with fists flying and no attempt at defense. The first two rounds of the fight were as furious and savage as any one at ringside had ever seen in their lives. Neither man would retreat.

When the bell rang for the third round, Terry McGovern, his face drawn with fury, rushed out of his corner determined to bring the match to an immediate close. So intent was he on rushing at his opponent that he came out wide open, his arms dangling at his sides.

The Omaha Kid was not one to pass up such an opportunity. He fired a terrific haymaker from his heels and caught the onrushing McGovern flush on his unprotected chin. Down went the champion in a heap, down and out! The Omaha Kid stepped back, looked at the fallen champion and then turned to the shocked fans at ringside. "Well?" he shouted. "Did I boast too much? Take a look at McGovern now!"

The referee, no less shocked than the ringsiders, had begun to toll the count over the stricken fighter. Slowly and deliberately, hesitating long between each number, the third man in the ring at last got to the count of eight. McGovern was still on the canvas, his face buried in resin dust, dead to the world. The referee fidgeted, hemmed and hawed. Six seconds passed before he uttered a grudging nine! That was as far as he would go. He seemed to have been hypnotized by the still form that lay at his feet.

"Count! Count!" screamed the frantic Omaha Kid. "Why don't you count him out?"

At this moment, one of McGovern's seconds shoved the referee aside and dumped half a bucket of ice water over the head of the fallen champion. The champion gasped at the shock and began feebly to move his arms and legs as though to rise.

"You're robbing me of the fight!" yelled the Omaha Kid to the referee. "What are you waiting for? He's been down for more than ten seconds. Why don't you count him out?"

McGovern twitched, then began to raise himself on rubbery legs. The referee backed away quickly.

The Omaha Kid watched the slowly rising McGovern and stepped forward eagerly. This time he wasn't going to leave anything to chance. He'd stow the champ away for good and the referee could count to a thousand before the guy would get up again.

Before the Omaha Kid could hit McGovern again, the champion suddenly pitched forward. As he fell he reached out and caught the Kid around the legs, clasping them tightly. Instinctively, McGovern began to haul himself up again, using his opponent's body as a ladder. The Omaha Kid frantically tried to shake himself free of the clawing arms. "Let go!" he yelled. "Hey, referee, make him let go!"

The referee had found something else to do at the moment and paid no attention to the Kid's appeal. Before he could do anything about it, Gardner heard the bell ending the round. Dejectedly he returned to his corner, convinced that nothing he could do would win the fight for him.

There are still oldtimers around who sat in on that memorable fight with watches in their hands. They'll tell you that McGovern was on the canvas for at least twenty seconds, and in the clinch that followed for thirty seconds more.

The Omaha Kid came out for the fourth round without the slightest desire to make a fight of it. Sparring half-heartedly, he ran into one of McGovern's really torrid punches and went down. The referee had no reason to stall this time. He counted to nine as briskly as the law allowed. The Omaha Kid staggered to his feet. Terrible Terry let go his famous right to the whiskers. That was the end of Oscar Gardner, the Omaha Kid.

All it adds up to is a one-line entry under a glorious record of a great champion. "Oscar Gardner, beaten by K.O. in four rounds." But it doesn't tell the whole story, does it?

A FIGHTER WHO WAS CAPABLE OF CALLING THE TURN WAS that fearsome little Barbadoes Demon, Joe Walcott, the 150-pounder who could lick heavyweights and often did. One day, matched with a promising white heavyweight, Joe found himself in the ring against two men when he learned that the referee was a close friend of his opponent. In the very first round, Joe crossed a right to the jaw and sent the big fighter to the canvas in a heap. The referee bent quickly over the fallen man, picked him up and propped him on his feet. Then, turning to the press row, the referee explained his action. "Sorry, gentlemen," he said. "That was just an accident. I tripped the fellow myself."

Joe Walcott chuckled at the amazing effrontery of the third man in the ring and stepped forward to resume the fight. He feinted, poked his left in the giant's face, and crossed another terrific right to the jaw, felling the big man like an ox in a slaughter house. Then he walked across the ring to the horrified arbiter. "Pardon me, Mister Referee," he said in a voice loud enough for the men in the press row to hear, "for the edification of mah frien's and mahself, would you be good enough to tell me, please, who in hell knocked him down that time?"

With a roar of laughter in his ears from the gentlemen of the press, the prejudiced referee could do only one thing. He counted out the fallen giant where he lay.

No DOUBT YOU'VE HEARD INNUMERABLE TALES OF A FIGHTER who knocked out an opponent in one round. You may even have heard of a fighter or two who knocked out his opponent twice in one round. But have you ever heard of the fighter who had to knock his opponent out five times in one round in order to win a fight?

One September day in 1920, Jimmy O'Gatty, welterweight, crawled through the ropes to fight a husky 175-

pounder. The fight took place in Glens Falls, New York. From the opening bell, little Jimmy O'Gatty punched his bigger and heavier opponent from pillar to post. The big man took everything for six bloody rounds. Then, in the seventh round, O'Gatty dropped his adversary with a terrific blow.

Ten seconds went by and still the pole-axed light heavyweight grovelled in the dust. Was O'Gatty declared the winner by a knockout? No. Was he even declared the winner, knockout or not? Not at all. The referee had not even begun to count over the stricken fighter. Instead, he calmly sat on the ropes in a corner waiting for the fallen warrior to climb to his feet and go on with the battle.

After some fifteen seconds, the groggy fighter rose on wobbly legs. Again O'Gatty sailed into him and knocked him off his feet. This time the big man stayed down for eleven seconds. Still there was no count. O'Gatty turned on the referee furiously.

"Why don't you count him out?" he demanded.

"Shut up!" replied the prejudiced referee. "I know my business. Go on and fight!"

Five times in that seventh round did Jimmy O'Gatty knock his opponent cold. The round lasted ten minutes, the longest, probably, in ring history. After the fifth knockout, the referee grudgingly awarded the decision to O'Gatty. There was no other choice since the big fellow on the floor was completely unconscious. The referee could have counted to ten thousand—slowly.

No story about James Johnston, the famous "Boy Bandit" of fistiana is more amusing than that of the first fight between Ted Kid Lewis, the sensational English fighter he managed, and Jack Britton, welterweight champion of the world managed by Dumb Dan Morgan.

The fistic records show that Jack Britton and Ted Kid Lewis met in the ring twenty-two times in all. The fights that followed the first one were anticlimactic. The initial meeting between the two fine welterweights was another story altogether.

The two men were matched, the first time, to go fifteen rounds to a referee's decision. The bout was to be held in the fair city of Boston.

On the day of the contest, Dumb Dan Morgan showed up not only with his champion, Jack Britton, but also with the referee who was to handle the fight, proving that the "Dumb" that went before the redoubtable manager's name was strictly a misnomer. When Jimmy Johnston heard about this, he said nothing. He waited until Jack Britton and Morgan's own referee were standing in the ring ready to begin. Then, Johnston leaped inside the ropes and, facing the gentlemen of the press who were seated around its edge, shouted lustily so that half of the spectators in the arena could hear, "Gentlemen! Gentlemen of the press, I want you to know that Morgan brought his own referee and this fight will not be decided on its merits!"

The referee, who heard all this clearly, glared across the ring at the red-faced little manager of the challenger. Jimmy Johnston took a deep breath and let out another burst. Pointing a trembling forefinger at the referee, he shouted, "This fellow is going to rob me!"

"You'll get a square deal!" protested the now angry official.

"Yes, I will!" shouted back Jimmy, louder than ever. "I've had experience with your kind before! Gentlemen, I want all you men to bear witness that Morgan and Britton have insulted the sportsmanship of Bostonians by bringing in an outsider to referee!"

Dan Morgan now entered the shouting contest. "Shut that Englishman up or I'll do it myself!" he roared. At the same time, Britton, as incensed as his manager, lunged after Ted Kid Lewis. In the mix-up, a Lewis punch knocked a Britton handler stone cold. A general melee followed and calm was restored only when a dozen policemen climbed between the ropes to stop the unscheduled fight so that the official one could begin.

With the clang of the very first bell, Jimmy Johnston began to shout at the referee in the middle of the ring. "He's robbing us! He's robbing us!"

On his part, the harassed referee kept retorting with, "Shut up, you loud-mouthed Englishman. I'm as honest as you'll ever be! You'll get a square deal."

As the rounds went by, the poor bewildered referee found himself spending more time denying his alleged dishonesty than looking at the fight he was supposed to judge.

In his corner, Dumb Dan Morgan sat viewing the proceedings with complete satisfaction. The unhappy Jimmy Johnston, in his corner, prayed and hoped that his man, Lewis, might come out of the contest with a draw.

At the end of the fight there was a loud buzz of speculation in the arena. Who had won the fight? No one was sure. Only the two managers felt that the decision was a foregone conclusion.

There was a moment's hesitation on the part of the referee. Then, to the accompaniment of a roar from the crowd, he walked across the ring and raised Ted Kid Lewis' hand in token of victory. Jimmy Johnston's boy had won! Dumb Dan Morgan nearly swooned. Jimmy Johnston was so shocked that he actually tumbled off the stool on which he was sitting.

The referee's decision did not bring the fight to a close, however. It was the signal for a resumption of fisticuffs that was fantastic to behold. The enraged Jack Britton flung himself at Ted Kid Lewis and the Englishman came back at him with both fists flying. For three minutes the two fighters stood toe to toe in a corner trading punches as the police, referee, handlers, and managers tried to separate them. Above the terrific racket only one voice could be heard. It was that of Jimmy Johnston, the Boy Bandit. He was yelling, "What's the squawk, fellows? The referee is an honest man! He called it as he saw it, that's all!"

By this time, the fans had entered wholeheartedly into the battle. Wooden seats were torn up. Beer bottles began to fly through the air and occasionally a dull clunk could be heard as glass found a target among the bobbing heads.

One hundred police stopped the Donnybrook. After a number of skulls were bounced against wooden clubs, the fighters were escorted to their dressing rooms. Here, in comparative privacy, the battle broke out anew. And still above the din, the dulcet tones of Johnston's voice could be heard. "Soreheads!" he cried. "Soreheads! The referee's an honest man! What's the squawk about anyhow?"

FISTIC PLACES TO REMEMBER

No fight champion ever hears mention of Madison Square Garden Bowl, located in Long Island City, New York, without thanking his stars that he will never have to fight there. Many champions have been dethroned in that open air arena. In its ten years of existence, it harbored the strangest jinx known to fistiana. Not one champion ever retained his title in Madison Square Garden Bowl!

The hoodoo started its work on the night of June 21, 1932 when the Bowl first opened. Sixty thousand fans were there to see heavyweight champion Max Schmeling meet Jack Sharkey for the title. And Boston Jack Sharkey won the crown!

Soon after, Sharkey crawled through the ropes in the Garden Bowl to defend his championship against Primo Carnera. In a weird fight, Carnera snatched the title away from Sharkey. The jinx was really taking hold.

The next Bowl fight saw champion Primo Carnera face the California madcap, Max Baer. The challenger slaughtered the big fellow. Once again the jinx had worked to defeat a champion.

Then the champion of the world battled a heavyweight has-been named Jim Braddock. Many believed that the challenger had been washed up for years before the fight. But Jim Braddock confused the experts and shocked the fans by licking Max Baer and winning the title. Once again the jinx of the Bowl held fast!

They never staged another heavyweight contest in that bowl because it came to be feared by all fighters as the graveyard of champions. Then baby-faced Jimmy McLarnin, welterweight champion of the world, laughed at the superstition and accepted a title match with challenger Barney Ross.

Sure enough, the jinx worked. McLarnin was shorn of his title. And to top it off, the two met again in the Madison Square Garden Bowl. The outcome? Champion Barney Ross lost his title to the challenger, Jimmy McLarnin!

When Ross, having rewon the title elsewhere again fought Henry Armstrong in the Bowl, the result was, as usual, a new champion!

Champion after champion took his title into the ill-fated Garden Bowl and came away from Long Island City a sadder and wiser man. Never once did any champion successfully defend his crown in that arena!

And in that jinxed boxing arena, a man also fought a ghost ring battle for the heavyweight championship of the world.

Years ago, Max Schmeling was matched to fight James J. Braddock for the heavyweight title. Almost on the eve of the big fight, James J. Braddock, because of circumstances beyond his control, refused to go through with the bout on the appointed night. Max Schmeling refused to accept the champion's excuse. When the day on which the fight had been scheduled finally arrived, Max Schmeling weighed in. That night at the appointed hour, he crawled through the ropes into the ring pitched in the center of Madison Square Garden Bowl to fight for the heavyweight championship of the world. It was a weird and ghostly sight, for in the ring there was no opponent to face Max Schmeling. The arena was silent and empty. All Max Schmeling did that evening was put in his appearance before an audience of 80,000 empty seats.

NO BANDIT EVER LEFT A TOWN MORE COMPLETELY LOOTED than Jack Kearns did when he was the manager of the great champion, Jack Dempsey. The town that Kearns picked clean was a little place called Shelby, in the sovereign state of Montana.

It seems that a pretty good heavyweight named Tom Gibbons was hot on the trail of the then champion of the world, Jack Dempsey. Kearns was smart enough to know that the fight, if arranged, would not amount to much. Gibbons was a fairly clever boxer but he was far from being a match for the fiery, hard-punching champion. Still, business was business. If any promoter felt sassy enough to put on the match, Kearns was willing to listen to reason, reason meaning money, of course.

Enthusiasm among the entrepreneurs was far from high. The fight did not promise to draw much at the gate, and the offers were none too liberal.

It was at this point in the proceedings that the little town of Shelby, Montana, stepped into the picture. Not satisfied with remaining the happy, prosperous little place that it was, Shelby sought fame and prominence in the world. The leading citizens of the town made a startling bid for the fight between Dempsey and Gibbons. For the defense of his title, Dempsey was offered $200,000 on the spot, and an additional $100,000 on the day of the fight.

No more welcome music had ever sounded in Jack Kearns' ears. The offer was snapped up before you could say sucker. The fight was set in Shelby for July 4, 1923. The townspeople congratulated themselves on the prize plum they had plucked from the fistic tree. Little did they know what misfortune they had brought down on themselves.

As the day of the fight approached, the people of Shelby, Montana, finally came to realize that they had overstepped themselves badly. The balance of money that was due to Kearns could not be raised.

On the eve of the fight, the local promoters came to Jack Kearns' hotel with their troubles. There was a fine sum of $43,000 available to pay him off; would it be enough?

Kearns sneered at the offer. He waved the contract before their faces and demanded the hundred thousand due him. They begged him to take what he could get and let the fight go on. Kearns said no money, no fight. The local folks said the town was stone broke. Kearns lit a fresh cigar. Voices began to rise. Words were said that might better have been left unsaid. A terrific battle followed, fists flew through the air, heads were conked. In the excitement, the sheriff of Shelby who was acting as chairman, got in the way of a stray bullet.

From all the ruckus Jack Kearns emerged triumphant, as usual. The town, at the end of its resources, somehow found the money to pay him off. The fight took place and it was a dull affair won by Dempsey on points. When it was over, Kearns and his crowd took the first train out of Shelby. Behind them they left a ruined, busted town. The leading bank had closed its doors. The citizens had lost their savings. It was a fearful price to pay for a bunch of soon-to-be-forgotten headlines.

SPARRING PARTNER

In the entire sport of boxing, there is no sadder figure than the lowly sparring partner. Never good enough to become a name fighter in his own right, the professional sparring partner wanders from fight camp to fight camp, serving as a human punching bag. He absorbs a brutal beating day after day, all for a few bucks. When he can no longer absorb the murderous beating for which he is hired, he is dumped on the fistic junkpile. That has always been the lot of the lowly and humble sparring partner. Still, there have been times when the human punching bag has dared the fates and had his moment of sports glory.

When Joe Louis was at his peak as champion, he had a great deal of trouble keeping sparring partners. One day, while preparing for the second Schmeling fight, a husky unknown came seeking a job with the great champion. He was hired at twenty-five bucks a day.

The stranger did not prove to be the usual catcher. Joe Louis just couldn't seem to put him on the floor. Not only that, when there was a furious mix-up in the middle of the ring, it was Joe Louis who caught a hard blow from the husky stranger and was dumped unceremoniously.

The next day, the sparring partner was out of a job. He was hastily paid off and told to beat it. He left, vowing that, somehow, somewhere, he would show the great Joe Louis and the rest of the world that he was a lot better than a sparring partner.

The years went by and the sparring partner who had been fired from Joe Louis' camp, tried to win fame in his own right. He wasn't very successful. For years he fought for handouts in shabby two-bit clubs. Four times he quit the ring in disgust. He was swindled, pushed around, ridiculed. He starved and hungered.

But his day came! It was in 1948 that the lowly sparring partner who had been thrown out of the champion's training camp stood again in a ring with the Brown Bomber. This time he was not there just to give Louis a workout. His name was Jersey Joe Walcott, and he was meeting Joe Louis for the heavyweight championship of the world!

That first Walcott-Louis fight was history-making. Walcott gave the champion the worst beating of his life, dropped him twice, and all but took the title from him. Even though he was not awarded the crown officially, many will tell you that Jersey Joe Walcott, ex-sparring partner, came out of that fight as the heavyweight champion of the world! The ex-human punching bag had dared defy the fates to have his moment of glory!

KID McCOY, ONE OF THE MOST UNUSUAL FIGHTERS IN THE history of the ring, ran away from home to seek his fortune at the tender age of twelve. After passing a few years in the hobo jungles, he became a fighter at eighteen. He was active in the ring from 1891 to 1922, a period of thirty-one years. It was he who originated the corkscrew punch.

He was one of the most skillful boxers ever to put on the gloves. He often fought men who outweighed him by as much as one hundred pounds, and beat them too. He also had quite a way with the ladies, marrying nine times in all! He spent years in jail as a convicted murderer. Then he died as he had lived, dramatically, for it was in a shabby hotel room in Detroit that Kid McCoy took his own life in 1941, leaving behind him a farewell note that read: "I can no longer stand the madness of the world."

As unusual as any of the facts in his colorful career was the way the Kid became a champion. He was working as a sparring partner for Tommy Ryan, who then held the middleweight title. Ryan was a tough, hard, flint-hearted fighting man. He gave Kid McCoy a bad time as sparring partner. The Kid was never given enough to eat. And when the hungry youngster was pushed into the ring to furnish Ryan a workout, the hard-hitting champion took particular pleasure in belting him.

Kid McCoy, however, was nobody's fool. He took the beatings without complaint, and with his eyes wide open. He vowed revenge against his cruel master. The Kid studied the champion's style closely and carefully, looked for the weakness in his defense, and catalogued every move the man made. After several weeks, the Kid thought he had learned all he needed to know to beat his tormentor. The problem now was to get him into the ring for a fight. The Kid solved this puzzle neatly.

First of all, he quit the training camp. Some time later, and apparently quite by accident, the champion ran into Kid McCoy on the street. The Kid was in rags, as shabby and unkempt as a hobo. His cheeks were pale and drawn. As he talked, he tried bravely to smother a hacking cough that seemed to shake every bone in his body.

"What graveyard did they dig you out of?" sneered the champion at his former sparring partner. "Man, you sure look like you're on your way out!"

McCoy coughed before he could reply. "Tom," he said weakly, "I'm really up against it. I've got to raise some money somehow. You've always been kind to me. Give me a break now, will you? A friend of mine who runs a club down on Long Island is willing to put me in the ring with

you. Look, we'll draw pretty good out there. You know
how the crowd likes you."

"Me get into the same ring with you?" roared the champ.
"You're crazy, Kid! I'd probably kill you with the first
punch. You're nothing now but a broken-down bum!"

"Please, Tom!" begged Kid McCoy. "You can make the
cut any way you want, even up to ninety per cent to the
winner. I'm willing to take a licking just to get a little
dough. "What do you say, champ, be a good guy!"

Ryan measured the pitiful wreck before him and snick-
ered. "All right, Kid," he said. "I guess I can do an old
pal a favor. Make it 90% to the winner, 10% to the loser,
and you're on!"

McCoy thanked the magnanimous champion and shuffled away, coughing and hacking for all he was worth.

The men met the next time in the ring pitched in Mas-
peth, Long Island. When Tommy Ryan walked into his
corner and looked across the ring, his jaw dropped at the
sight before him. There was Kid McCoy all right. But
what a different-looking Kid McCoy this was! No healthier
specimen had ever stepped into the ring. McCoy sneered
across the ring at the baffled champion. And Ryan knew
at once that he had been tricked by his former sparring
partner.

He foamed with rage at the trick. He had barely gone
through the motions in training for this fight. Still—he'd
give that fresh punk the lesson of his life. He'd show him
that fooling the champ with a dash of powder on the cheeks,
some borrowed old clothes and a fake cough was dangerous business.

But Kid McCoy had planned his revenge carefully. The
fight that followed the opening bell was a vicious one. Mc-
Coy cut Ryan to ribbons with a splashing attack but deliberately refused to land the blow that would put Ryan
to sleep for good. With every cutting swipe the Kid whis-

pered some taunt or insult that inflamed the champion. Not a single injury done him in the past did McCoy overlook in his single-minded purpose. A cruel left hook would thud into the champion's bloody face and McCoy would sneer, "That's for the bad food you gave me." A right cross would cut another gash in Ryan's cheek and McCoy would whisper, "That's for the hard bed you had me sleep in." A jab to Ryan's puffed-up eye would be followed by, "And that's for all the lickings you handed me."

Few fighters in all fistiana were ever on the receiving end of a beating like the one Tommy Ryan took from the Kid whose right name was Norman Selby. No one ever took a sweeter revenge. And, to top it off, Kid McCoy coolly collected 90% of the purse while the battered bleeding Tommy Ryan picked up the loser's end of 10%.

WHEN JIM CORBETT WAS WORLD'S HEAVYWEIGHT CHAMPION, a big, lumbering ox of a man from Carroll, Ohio, came to

the training camp to serve as a sparring partner. The new man was rugged and he was strong, with the punch of a mule in either fist.

Corbett was riding high at the time, for was he not the man who had licked the great John L. Sullivan and shorn him of his title? Corbett hired the lumbering ox with a lordly wave of the hand and stepped into the roped-off arena with him.

The new sparring partner served the clever champion well for a few days. Then, the big ox forgot himself and the reputation of the champion. He began to push Gentleman Jim around. Infuriated at what he considered a personal insult, champion Corbett fired his new sparring partner on the spot.

Now it was the sparring partner's turn to get sore. As he packed his few belongings, he came over to the champion and said, "Corbett, some day soon, I'm going to wear that heavyweight crown of yours!"

It seemed a ridiculous boast, for how could that clumsy oaf of a giant ever hope to win the most coveted crown in fistiana?

A year later, Corbett lost his title to the Australian blacksmith, Bob Fitzsimmons. The new champion, in his first defense of the crown, met—you guessed it—Corbett's old sparring partner. And, to cap it all, the sparring partner took the title away from Fitzsimmons. The new champion, the sparring partner of only a short time before, had made good his boast. After less than a dozen fights in the ring, Jim Jeffries, the big lumbering ox who had been fired as sparring partner by Jim Corbett, was champion of the world!

PARIS IN THE SPRINGTIME

For a few years after the end of the career of Gorgeous Georges Carpentier, the boxing game in France fell on evil times. There was no fighter of French birth to make any stir in the ring. Then, suddenly and seemingly out of nowhere, a new heavyweight sprang into prominence. His name was André Lenglet.

Parisians went wild over Lenglet. He was a handsome devil, colorful, classy, and with a fierce will to fight his way to the top.

As André Lenglet made his climb, all France acclaimed him as the fighter who would bring back the glorious days of Carpentier, greatest fighter and sports hero in the land. It was with high hopes that they wished him well as, in 1936, young Lenglet left for the United States to seek further fame and fortune.

For two years, André fought in the American prize ring, meeting all comers. Among the leading heavies he defeated were Hans Birkie, Al McCoy, Marty Gallagher, Alberto Lovell, Ray Impellitiere and Buddy Baer. With every fight, André Lenglet punched his way closer and closer to the objective he sought—a match for the heavyweight championship of the world.

And then came World War II. Without a moment's hesitation, André threw together his things and returned to his native France.

Nothing more was heard of the promising young heavy-

weight for some time. Then, during the darkest days of the
conflict a young flyer on leave in the United States re-
counted a strange story he brought back from the other
side.

In a dreary, deserted sidewalk café somewhere in the
south of France, André Lenglet sat at a table, alone with
his gloomy thoughts. As a man passed the café, André idly
raised his head. The man was ragged, unkempt, worn and
weary. But the big frame on which the flesh hung so loose-
ly showed that this had once been a magnificent figure of
a man. André's eyes widened. He recognized him. It was
his boyhood hero, Georges Carpentier.

"Monsieur Carpentier!" called Lenglet, waving his arm
at the passing man. "Won't you join me for a little glass?
I'm André Lenglet, don't you remember me?"

Carpentier accepted the invitation and seated himself
opposite his host. André Lenglet stared at him with un-
believing eyes. Carpentier chuckled ruefully as he noticed
the shock in the other's face. "You seem surprised at my
appearance, old man. I'm an ugly sight, eh, André?"

"But—but what's happened?" asked Lenglet, fumbling
for words. "You who were once so famous, so rich?"

Carpentier laughed harshly, then said, "The Nazis, my
friend. When they came to Paris I lost everything, but
naturally. I escaped, as you see, leaving behind me all my
money, my beautiful café, my apartment houses, in a word,
everything! Now I work at odd jobs, wherever I can find
them, for a few measly francs, if I do not wish to starve."
Carpentier hesitated, brooding, before going on more cheerfully. "But you, André, you mustn't despair. You're still
a young man. You, at least, can fight again. How often I
saw you in the ring! You were a great fighter!"

Then, as though suddenly struck by a bright idea, Carpentier began to speak with great rapidity. "André, I have
it! How would you like to fight in the ring again? Why,

don't we both make a comeback? You will do the fighting and I, I will manage and train and teach you everything I know. We'll go back to the United States and make a lot of money between us, eh, André? I know all the ropes, believe me. Was I not once the light-heavyweight champion of the world, I, Georges Carpentier? That's it, old man. It's our big chance for a comeback, mine and yours!"

André Lenglet shrugged and shook his head sadly. "No, Monsieur Carpentier," he said. "I think not. I've been in the war and. . ."

"Nonsense!" snapped back Georges Carpentier. "I too was in a war when I was a fighter and came out an even greater hero because of it. I tell you, André, if you let me manage you, I can get you a fight for the heavyweight title. Have you not always wished to meet the world's champion in the ring? It's a great thrill, André, believe me. Did I not meet the great Jack Dempsey before 90,000 people for the title? I'll make you a champion, André! You can't miss, I swear it!"

André sat quietly plucking at his lower lip as Carpentier leaned forward more insistently than ever. "I repeat, André, it's the chance for a comeback for both of us. Look here, you fought Jack Roper and he got to fight Joe Louis, did he not? You beat Buddy Baer and he too later met Joe Louis and almost won the title. You can do it, André. We'll both come back!"

"Alas, no, Monsieur Carpentier, you do not understand," said André Lenglet at last. Speaking, the young man slowly rose to his feet and moved away from the table.

Georges Carpentier, about to go on with his plea, stopped talking and his mouth fell open in shocked surprise. André Lenglet, the prizefighter who might have become heavyweight champion of the world, had paid his price to war. He now had but one leg.

No AMERICAN WHO WENT TO PARIS BETWEEN THE TWO World Wars could miss hearing of the fabulous sports promoter with the familiar and homely name of Jefferson Davis Dickson. The name was not a phony for Dickson was a true American born and bred who had been raised in no less an American city than Natchez, Mississippi. Had there not been a first World War, it is very likely that the name of Jeff Dickson would have become as well-known to American sports fans as that of Tex Rickard.

It was as a doughboy that Jeff Dickson first set foot on the friendly soil of France. Once there, nothing could tear him away from his beloved Paris. With an unusual flair for the spectacular Jeff Dickson became a sports promoter. One of his stunts was to promote a pretty golden-haired girl from Norway as a sensational dancer on ice. And how successful that stunt was! The girl with the golden hair became in time the most glamorous attraction in sports history, Sonja Henie!

But boxing was Jeff Dicksons' first love. All the big fights in Europe were put on by him. It was under his aegis that a lumbering and unknown circus roustabout named Primo Carnera made his debut in the ring.

In Paris, Dickson built the *Palais de Sport*, a monument to his promotional genius. It was there Jeff Dickson first introduced the sport of hockey.

Jeff Dickson might have spent the rest of his life in his beloved Paris if the Germans hadn't burst into ugly action again. The Nazis conquered France and ran Dickson out of his beloved *Palais de Sport*. With sadness in his heart, Dickson beat a retreat to his native land. But he couldn't remain inactive for long. Despite his age—he was forty-seven years old—Jeff Dickson went into the air force as captain. No Mississippian, suh, could stay out of a fight.

He was sent abroad to do photographic intelligence work in combat bombers. One day his plane was shot down. The War Department listed Jeff Dickson as killed in action! "Captain Jefferson Davis Dickson was shot down in flames and lost his life during a mission not far from—Paris." Jeff Dickson was still trying to get back to his beloved boulevards and the *Palais de Sport*.

THEY LIVE BY THEIR WITS

Something went out of boxing when the final bell sounded for little Jimmy Johnston, the "Boy Bandit," at the ripe age of seventy. The little man with the sharp twinkling eyes, the witty tongue, the fertile brain, and the rakish derby hat will be sorely missed. No more colorful character has even been connected with the prize ring than Jimmy Johnston.

He was a kid out of Liverpool, England, who arrived in this country at the age of sixteen with the intention of becoming a prize fighter. He proved to be a fair-to-middling bantamweight about half a century ago. However, one day little Jimmy Johnston was offered the sum of twenty-five dollars to fight Terry McGovern. Before accepting, Jimmy dropped in to the gym to watch the ferocious flyweight champion work. One look was more than enough for the sharp little Englishman. "Why should I fight McGovern for twenty-five dollars?" he asked. "I've got twenty-five dollars. Besides, a man with my brains should take no chances of having them scattered on a ring floor."

Jimmy Johnston quit the ring. As a manager, he really began to live. His fertile and ingenious mind made it possible for him to get more out of mediocre stumble-bums than any other manager in the history of boxing. Under his guidance, second-rate fighters became glamorous. Jimmy knew how to dress them up to look like somebody.

Once he found a giant from South Africa named Boer

Rodel. This character had been fighting in London and Paris prize rings with middling success. When Jimmy got his hands on him, he promptly rigged him out in an old brown army overcoat which he bought in a pawnshop and began to ballyhoo Rodel as a hero of the Boer War. That was in 1912. Of course, it didn't matter to the wily Jimmy that his fighter, Boer Rodel, was only twenty-four and that the Boer War had been over for thirteen years. Johnston made a neat fortune with Boer Rodel.

Another time, the larcenous little Johnston found himself an unknown Welshman named Bill Daniels. Having sized up the situation, Johnston spent a dime for a red bandanna handkerchief, another ten cents for a pair of cheap earrings, and transformed the Welshman into Gypsy Daniels, a romantic character from the Rhondda Mountains, the king of the gypsies, no less! It didn't matter that Daniels couldn't fight a lick. Jimmy Johnston made another fine bit of change with him.

Aside from laughs, though, let it not be forgotten that Jimmy Johnston handled more world's champions than any other manager in history. There were seven of them, including Jem Driscoll, Ted Kid Lewis, Harry Greb, Johnny Dundee, Pete Latzo, Vince Dundee, and Mike Mc-Tigue. There were many more who were contenders, but never made the very top.

In spite of this imposing record, it was a bitter blow to Jimmy that he never had a heavyweight champion of the world under his wing. It wasn't for lack of trying. Jimmy hunted high and low for a big boy good enough to take the title but one after the other they failed him. He piloted big Abe Simon into a fight with Joe Louis and saw his man get knocked out. He found a rugged college lad named Bob Pastor and twice saw him fail to lift the crown.

Shortly before his death, Jimmy Johnston was honored with a plaque for his long years of service to boxing. The honor was richly deserved and I'm sure Jimmy appreciated it, but I'll bet he would have swapped it willingly for a big husky youngster who could be brought along for the heavyweight championship of the world!

THERE HAVE BEEN FEW CHAMPIONS IN MODERN TIMES WHO did not have behind them the sometimes shadowy, sometimes prominent, figure of the man known as the boxing manager. Not the least colorful of these managers is Joe Gould, the fellow who led a washed-up and poverty-stricken dock worker from obscurity to the very pinnacle of success, the world's heavyweight championship.

It was a couple of decades ago that Joe Gould, then a small-time boxing manager, tried to peddle to the boxing trade a promising light heavyweight named Harry Galfund. Gould was attempting to sell the fighter's contract for twenty-five hundred dollars. The men who were to buy it dropped into the gym to see the young man put on the gloves before closing the deal. Joe Gould arrived with his fighter. Looking around for a possible sparring partner Joe saw an unknown Irish kid working out alone in a corner. He called the kid over and snapped, "Hey, kid, do you want to put on the gloves with my boy for a couple of rounds? There's a five-dollar bill in it for you."

The five-spot must have looked pretty big to the unknown boy for he hopped right into the ring and went to work on Joe Gould's promising fighter. The fight went one round and the kid almost murdered Galfund. The result was that the prospective buyers shook their heads and went away. Galfund's contract wasn't worth a plugged nickel. Sadly, Joe Gould came up to the Irish kid and said, "I ought to crown you with a club, you dumb Irishman. You just knocked me out of a small fortune." Gould hesitated, then smiled. "But you're a comer, kid. How would you like me to manage you?"

"Sure," grinned the Irish kid. "My name's Braddock, Jim Braddock."

The chance meeting was the beginning of an amazing fight story and an enduring friendship. At first, Jim Braddock went up fast. With his terrific punch he captured the fancy of the boxing world. He fought and licked some good fighters. Always at his side was his pal and manager, shrewd little Joe Gould. They made money. Things were good for both of them. Then one night, Jim Braddock broke his right hand. It healed eventually, but the turning point in his career had been reached. Braddock began to slip. He lost more and more fights. Finally he was all washed up—and broke as well.

Unable to get any fights, Jim Braddock went out looking for other jobs. He tended bar, worked on the docks as a stevedore, did anything he could to support a wife and three children. His little manager still stuck to him, giving him what he could though it wasn't much. Joe Gould was broke too.

Those were dark days for Jim Braddock but his pal and manager kept the spark of hope alive. "Jim," he would say, "you're not finished. We'll move back to the top. Just wait and see. I'm working on it all the time, seeing a lot of guys. I'll get a fight for you and we'll be in the dough again!"

Then one day, little Joe Gould came running in excitement to his pal to tell him about a fight he had signed for. It was against the sensational new heavyweight, Corn Griffin, touted as the coming champion of the world. It looked like murder to match old Jim Braddock against the promising youngster. But Joe Gould had faith in his friend. Braddock knocked out the new sensation. And, when Joe shouted after the fight that now they were well on their way to the championship of the world, Jim Braddock believed him.

And Joe was right. Not long after the Griffin fight, the doughty little manager got his man into the ring against champion Max Baer for the heavyweight title. The odds were twenty-to-one against Braddock. No one believed he could last more than a few rounds with the hard-hitting champion. That is, no one but Gould and Braddock. And how wrong the smart guys were. Braddock won the title from the fading Baer and made a Cinderella story come true. In one year Jim Braddock, helped by his pal and manager, Joe Gould, rose from rags to riches, from oblivion to world fame!

Bringing a man from obscurity to the top is a serious and difficult grind, but Joe Gould has had his share of laughs. One of his best memories goes far back to the time when Tex Rickard was the top man among the fight promoters.

It was about three o'clock one morning when Joe Gould's phone rang. Tex Rickard was on the phone and he wanted Joe at his office at once. Gould got into his clothes and ran for a cab.

As soon as Rickard saw Gould he shouted to him across the room, "Hey, Joe, I'm in a spot. I need someone to fight Angel Firpo in Havana. You've got a boy named Italian Jack Herman. Do you want to go down to Havana with him to meet Firpo?"

"Sure, Tex," replied Joe without a moment's hesitation. "We'll leave in the morning."

The contract was hastily drawn up. Herman and Gould's end of the purse was to be $5,000. And Joe rushed out of Rickard's office to find his fighter. He had forgotten that he had not seen his boy for several months and didn't even know whether the boxer was alive.

Gould began to search frantically since he was working

against time. Finally, after several hours, he traced Herman to a rooming house in Hoboken. At five in the morning, Joe was banging on the door. At last, a sleepy landlady poked out her head and demanded to know what Joe wanted at this ungodly hour.

"Where's Jack Herman?" screamed Joe. "I got to see him right away!"

"Go away," replied the angry landlady. "He's in the hospital. He's been there for weeks!"

Shocked by the information, but not at all dismayed, Joe Gould dashed for the local hospital and bribed his way to Jack Herman's room. The fighter was sound asleep. Joe shook him vigorously. "Jack!" he shouted. "Jack, wake up!"

Herman woke with a start, to see the wild-eyed Joe Gould leaning over him. "What are you doing here?" gasped Herman. "Am I dying or something?"

"Don't be silly!" snapped Joe. "This is no time to die. Come on, get up, we got to go to Havana to fight Àngel Firpo on Sunday. Hurry up, you sap, we got to catch a train!"

Jack Herman shook his head mournfully. "I can't go," he whispered. "I can't fight, Joe. I got a pain in the belly. The doc says I got appendicitis, maybe."

"Appendicitis, he says!" yelled Gould. "Are you out of your mind? For $5,000, how can you afford to have appendicitis?"

The reluctant Jack Herman dutifully climbed out of bed and got dressed. Joe Gould got him to the train in time and tenderly tucked him into bed. Hearing that ice was good for appendicitis, he instructed Jack to keep a good-sized pack on his tummy, and keep buying as much as he needed for the trip.

Italian Jack Herman made it to Havana and finally got into the ring for his match against Àngel Firpo. For all his heroic measures, Joe took a bad beating. Firpo knocked his boy out in the second round but the $5,000 purse did a little to soothe the wily manager.

Then came the totting up of expenses. One item hit Joe Gould right between the eyes. It read: "Ice—$260." Joe yelled for Jack Herman and asked how come.

"You told me," said the innocent Herman. "I bought all that ice to put on my belly for the appendicitis."

"Why, you bum!" screamed Joe Gould. "For 260 clams you can buy a whole iceberg! What are you trying to hand me?"

"I don't care what you think," answered Jack. "I needed ice for my appendicitis and $260 it is. That stuff melts, you know!"

Joe Gould had to give in and pay for the ice out of his own share of the purse. And it was only months later that Tex Rickard found out that smart little Joe Gould had pawned off on him a sick fighter kidnapped from a hospital. It was much too late to do anything about it then.

OF ALL THE HEAVYWEIGHT CHAMPIONS IN HISTORY, IT IS generally thought that Jack Johnson was the cleverest, certainly as a defensive boxer. There was one little trick of his that used to make the fight fans ooh and aah when they saw it, and that was his uncanny ability to pick off the punches of his opponent in mid-air. Johnson could actually catch the fastest blows on his glove tips. Many people have wondered how Li'l Artha ever developed that remarkable knack. You may be sure that the fighter was not born with that great defense of his. It was acquired because of a good friend's reluctance to take a beating, and it happened long before Johnson became the great champion he was.

Jack Johnson was a stevedore on the New Orleans docks.

He was miserably poor. At the end of a hard day's work, it was Johnson's custom to shuffle off to a shabby wind-blown shack owned by a good friend of his named Sam Pruitt. Pruitt had once been a fighter noted for his ter-rific sock, but had retired from the ring to a more peaceful life.

Sam Pruitt was fond of his friend, Jack Johnson, and set himself up as a sort of manager, trainer and time-keeper for the big fellow who used his friend's home as his gymnasium. Often enough, Johnson and Pruitt put on the gloves for a bout. Li'l Artha of course would wallop the little fellow from wall to wall.

The friend, though, took it all in stride, happy in the knowledge that Jack Johnson was well on his way to be-coming a first-class fighting man. A blissful grin would cross his battered face as he dreamed of Jack as the fu-ture champion of the world. The hardest blows seemed to be worth it with such a prospect in view.

In those early days, Jack Johnson had already acquired the fun-loving habits that spread his name around the world when he became champion. Many an evening he would step out on the town, have a barrel of fun, then re-turn late at night with some drunken friends and pound on poor Sam Pruitt's door for admittance.

Little Sam would wake up from a sound sleep, admit the buoyant Johnson and his mob and then reluctantly put on the boxing gloves for a session with the giant for the amusement of the boisterous crowd. As usual, Johnson would pound his friend from pillar to post. At the end of these special early-morning set-to's Johnson would fling a silver dollar to his battered friend as payment for his services as sparring partner.

After this had happened a number of times, Sam Pruitt began to take stock of the situation. He felt that if he were to live to a ripe old age, something would have to be done about it. The daily beatings he was receiving at the hands of the burly giant, Jack Johnson were getting to be too much for him.

He thought of a plan at last. The next day after a particularly savage beating, Pruitt drew on the boxing gloves slowly and spoke up to the silent Johnson. "Artha," he said, "I do like you, and I'm sure willing to give you all the work you need. I'm the man to see you become a great fighter, you can bet on that. Now, Artha, I've decided you hit hard enough. That's all taken care of. Now I'm gonna make you so clever nobody is gonna be able to lay a hand on you. And to do that, here's how we're going to work from now on. I'll do all the hitting and swinging, and you just do the blocking and ducking. That is the absolute sure-pop best practice there is to learn how to be real clever in the ring!"

Big Jack Johnson was agreeable, and for months and months thereafter, the hard-hitting little fellow fired away with terrific punches at the other man. Johnson would merely stand opposite the little guy, grinning and blocking every punch flung at him or picking it off in mid-air.

So well did Jack Johnson learn this difficult feat that no fighter in the world, however great, was able fully to penetrate the armor-like defense he threw up. And yet he learned it, not to save himself from punishment in the ring but because a little friend of his wanted to save his own hide.

As CLEVER A MANAGER AS JACK KEARNS WAS, THERE WAS ONE occasion on which the wily money-maker out-smarted himself. This happened when Jack took Mickey Walker to Louisville for a little fun and the Kentucky Derby.

Kearns and Walker arrived in the horse country a few days before the big race. Once there, somebody sold the wily Doc a bill of goods, talking him into sending his pet against a palooka named Paul Swiderski on the eve of the Derby. It sounded like a good proposition. Pitting the great Mickey Walker against a soft third-rater ought to give the crowd a lot of fun, a few laughs, and the thrill of watching the Toy Bulldog stow away an opponent. There was, besides, the matter of picking up some easy dough. Yes, the setup looked like a natural. Doc Kearns smiled with contentment. The deal made, he went out looking for some easy sucker money and found it by betting his entire bank roll on Walker to win by a knockout.

Fun-loving Mickey Walker was a natural fighter and never one to bother much about training. Without giving the coming encounter the least bit of thought, Mickey set out to have the time of his life. Hours before the fight he was in a gay spot somewhere in Louisville, stuffing himself with the finest of rich food, and washing it down with copious drafts of the choicest liquid refreshment.

When he crawled through the ropes that night, Mickey

Walker looked like a stuffed pig. As the bell rang, he waddled out to the center of the ring, lifted one hand with difficulty and then the roof fell in on him. Sock! Bang! Plop! The proud Mickey Walker was down, stretched at full length in the resin, while the third-rater, Paul Swiderski, was standing in his corner grinning broadly as the referee began to chant the fatal count.

There was a reason why Mickey Walker was called the Toy Bulldog. When the count reached nine, the groggy fighter brushed away the cobwebs and dragged himself to his tottering feet. Again he staggered into an explosion of fists that dropped him to the canvas. Up went Mickey. Down went Mickey. Up went Mickey. Down went Mickey.

Seven times in that first round did Swiderski floor the groggy, punch-drunk Toy Bulldog. And then, suddenly and unexpectedly, the bell ending the round sounded. At the same moment, Teddy Hayes, Walker's trainer, leaped inside the ropes and for no reason at all, crossed the ring and took a punch at Swiderski's manager. A free-for-all started promptly. In a moment, all the seconds, the trainers, and an assortment of Louisville police were in the ring pummeling and being pummeled in a wild disorder.

While the rumpus was going on, Kearns was in the corner with Walker working feverishly over the dazed Bulldog. For fifteen long precious minutes the wild melee went on. Order was finally restored by the police.

But the plan—if it was a plan—had worked to perfection. Kearns had Mickey Walker in fair shape again. The Toy Bulldog fought the rest of the fight, purely by instinct. Game as he was, the tenacious Walker managed to squeeze out a close decision. It was one of the gamest comebacks ever seen.

No sooner had Mickey Walker reached his dressing room than the enraged Swiderski, furious because the referee had, in his opinion, cheated him out of a victory, took a few more punches at the Bulldog. This time Doc Kearns as well as trainers, seconds and police took part in the battle that followed. For almost half an hour the struggle raged in the dressing room and the corridor outside. Poor Mickey Walker, still dazed, bloody and groggy from the fight he had fought in the ring, now found himself fighting with similar fury outside it. Although practically out on his feet, he kept socking anything that loomed up before him, be it Swiderski henchman, Louisville police, or his own trainer!

At the end, dozens lay stretched out cold by Mickey Walker's fists. Order was again restored. Peaceful quiet again fell on the Louisville front. Everything was fine now, except for the fact that both Kearns and Walker were stone broke. Kearns had lost his entire bankroll which had been wagered on a Walker victory by a knockout. The two men borrowed money to get them out of town. It was a night that they would never forget, that night in Louisville when Jack Kearns lost all his money by betting on a sure thing that couldn't miss, and almost lost his life as well.

PRIZE FIGHTING IS A TOUGH GAME AND MANY OF THE CHARACTERS who move along Cauliflower Alley aren't exactly saints. The common belief is that the worst of them all is the average manager. It is true that most of them are hard-boiled sharpshooters who have all too little interest in the boys who fight under their management except for the dough they can make out of them. But sometimes a prizefight manager comes along who's a bit different. Like Phil Schlossberg.

For many years Phil Schlossberg served in the United States Navy. He was a gob with a pair of handy fists, good enough to help him win the heavyweight championship of the service. Not only was he a hero in the ring, he was a hero under actual fire, too, for Phil won the Navy Cross for valor during the first World War.

On completing his long tour of service, Phil happened to come across a nice, handsome, husky youngster named Ernie Schaaf. Schaaf wanted to be a fighter. Schlossberg knew a lot about ring warfare. The two men became fast friends, and Phil became Ernie's manager. He had great faith in the lad's ability and predicted that he would go places with his fists.

Phil Schlossberg was right, too, for Ernie Schaaf proved quite a battler. Up and up he went in the heavyweight ranks until there began to be talk that Ernie was on the way to the championship.

As soon as Ernie Schaaf became prominent in fistiana, wise and influential guys tried to muscle in on the new heavyweight prospect. A lot of pressure was brought to bear on Phil to sell his contract to a big-time manager with a better "in" to the big things. The pressure was too strong to withstand. Phil Schlossberg sold Schaaf's contract for ten thousand dollars.

On the day they parted, the best of friends, Phil took Ernie aside and gave him a heart-to-heart talk. "I love you like my own son," he said. "Maybe it is better that someone else manage you from here on, someone with more influence. You're a great fighter, Ernie, and with the right breaks you're going to be the champion of the world. I don't want to stand in your way. There's only this, Ernie. Now that you're getting into the big time, a lot of things can happen to you. Watch your step. You might even get hurt in the ring, so be careful. Good luck, son, I'll always be on the sidelines rooting for you."

Ernie Schaaf was deeply touched by his former manager's words. And, as a farewell gesture of esteem, he begged his old friend to take out an insurance policy of $10,000 on Schaaf's life. Phil Schlossberg did so.

Then, one day, not long after, poor Ernie Schaaf was killed in the ring after absorbing a terrific beating from huge Primo Carnera. Ernie had gone into that fight feeling unwell. He did his best but it cost him his life.

Upon Ernie Schaaf's death, his former manager, Phil Schlossberg naturally collected the $10,000 on the policy he held on the dead fighter's life. The money was all his, and he certainly had need of it at the time.

But Phil was made of different stuff than that usually found in a boxing manager. Instead of stowing the dough away in his bank account, Phil grabbed the first train for Boston with the check. There he handed the entire sum of $10,000 to Ernie Schaaf's mother. It was as touching and gallant a gesture as ever took place in the rough, tough sport of boxing.

WHEN GEORGES CARPENTIER ARRIVED IN THIS COUNTRY FOR his historic heavyweight championship fight with Jack Dempsey, he set up training quarters at Manhasset, Long Island, with a great deal of secrecy and mystery. The cover-up operation of the challenger was all part of the big bally-hoo for the fight that was to draw the first million dollar gate in history.

One day, "Philadelphia Jack" O'Brien, esteemed as one of the most scientific boxers of his era, penetrated the aura of mystery around the camp and dropped in for a visit. O'Brien, who was a perfect gentleman and the Gene Tunney of his day, sought out Gus Wilson, Carpentier's trainer, with a proposition that he had in mind. He had come, he said, to give the visiting Frenchman the benefit of his own great ring experience.

Gus Wilson was only too glad to accept the offer. Who

could teach his fighter more than the clever Philadelphia Jack?

O'Brien drew Carpentier aside after meeting him. "Look, my boy," he said to him in a low whisper, "I've got some vital information for you as to how to fight Dempsey. Now, first of all, it won't do you the least bit of good to hit Dempsey on the chin or on the body, in the middle. He's as hard as a rock." And O'Brien shook his head dolefully at the thought of Dempsey's hard middle and chin.

"But what, then, am I to do, monsieur?" asked the puzzled Carpentier. "Where am I to hit him?"

"There's just one vulnerable spot on Dempsey," replied O'Brien, "and that's on the throat—like this." And, as he said the last words, O'Brien opened his hand with the thumb widely extended, and poked Carpentier sharply just below the Adam's apple. The Frenchman let out a gasp, then began to strangle and cough.

"You see what it does?" cried out the delighted O'Brien. "Like I told you, poke him that way." And again he hit the Frenchman in exactly the same and by now tender spot. The poor Carpentier really began to choke and splutter.

Gus Wilson, the trainer, hearing the racket, rushed to the scene. "Hey," he shouted, "what's going on in here?"

Philadelphia Jack laughed. "Nothing, Gus," he said with an airy flip of the hand, "I was just showing your man how to beat Dempsey."

Gus took another look at the doubled-up and red-faced Carpentier who was still struggling for breath. "Oh, yeah?" growled the suspicious trainer. "Look what you done to him. He's nearly knocked out right now. Get out of here, O'Brien!"

Philadelphia Jack O'Brien shrugged and went on his way without further ado. During the night Carpentier woke, groaning with pain. "My throat," he croaked, "it hurts. I cannot swallow. I am ruined."

For two days, Gorgeous Georges' throat ached and pained so much that he could swallow only broth and milk. And in the meantime, a great light began to dawn on trainer Gus Wilson. He discovered that O'Brien was a good friend of Jack Kearns, manager of Jack Dempsey. And he realized that they had played him for a sucker, nearly ruining his fighter before the bout had even begun.

Jack Dempsey, as it turned out, needed no tricks to beat Georges Carpentier. Brought to the arena in Jersey City an hour before fight time by a special police escort, Dempsey was taken by Tex Rickard to look at the immense crowd that filled Boyle's Thirty Acres.

"Jack," said the great promoter, "just look at that crowd. That's the greatest thing that ever happened to the boxing game. Just think of it, nearly 90,000 people and the first million dollar gate in history! Now, Jack, you have to do me a great favor. This Carpentier is a nice fellow. Be careful and don't kill him. I mean that, Jack. If you kill him, all this will be ruined. Boxing will die on the spot. Just take it easy and knock him out when you get ready. If everything goes off all right, there will be many more million dollar gates. We'll make a lot of money, Jack. So promise me you won't savage the guy, just knock him out clean and easy."

Jack Dempsey dispatched Georges Carpentier to the land of slumber by a clean knockout in four rounds. And the boom in boxing was on, with many million dollar gates to follow this first one. Tex Rickard was certainly a far-seeing man.

ANOTHER CLEVER OPERATOR IN THE BOXING GAME WAS OLD Doc Bagley. He, too, found it impossible to appreciate the qualities of a certain studious heavyweight. This time, however, Doc actually had the big fellow under contract

and wanted only to get rid of him. Somebody foolishly offered Doc two thousand dollars for the contract and Doc
grabbed it. In return, the fighter proceeded to win the
heavyweight championship of the world, retire undefeated,
and rest easy under the responsibility of a very comfort-
able fortune earned in the ring. In fact, the big man picked
up $990,000 for the thirty minutes he spent in the ring
in his last fight. His name was Gene Tunney.

The biggest blunder, though, may have been the one
made by Jimmy Johnston, known far and wide in the boxing world as the "Boy Bandit." It seems that one day a
seedy-looking hobo blew into New York and begged Jimmy to manage him. But the "Boy Bandit" had seen the
ragged hobo in his first ring appearance against a second-
rate mug some time before, and had seen said mug give
the hobo the licking of his life. So he laughed in derision.
"Go 'way," he said. "I can't waste any time with a bum
like you."

Unfortunately, Jimmy Johnston lived to regret his
words. He had fumbled the biggest pot of gold in boxing.
The ragged hobo became the most sensational heavyweight
champion of the world, Joe Louis not excluded, earning a
fortune of ten million dollars, and making his name, Jack
Dempsey, the most famous in the world of fisticuffs.

JOE JACOBS IS GONE NOW, BUT THE PICTURESQUE CHARACTER
of the little man with the big cigar still lives in the hearts
of the men who frequent Cauliflower Alley. And for all
the laughs and jokes and shrewd gags he pulled in his lifetime, there is still a lot of solid substance in Yussel Jacobs'
career as manager of prize fighters.

Little Joe was as quick-witted, as bold and imaginative
as any man ever connected with the ring. No one will forget his weird but enduring phrases, "We wuz robbed!"

and "I shudda stood in bed." And the stories told about the wonderful little guy are enduring proof of his cleverness.

After Mike McTigue won the championship from Battling Siki in Dublin on St. Patrick's Day, Joe Jacobs did a complete switch and put McTigue on a spot similar to the one Siki had stood on. He took bold Michael to Columbus, Georgia, to fight the pride of the South, Young Stribling. However, Yussel took one small precaution. He brought along his own referee.

The bout was a very close one, and McTigue was awarded the decision. After the fight, a big mob of local fans let their emotions get the better of their sportsmanship to the extent of surrounding the hotel in which Jacobs and McTigue were staying. The cry went up to hang the little manager for having stolen the decision from the rightful winner, Stribling.

The little guy with the big cigar didn't scare so easily. Calmly, he faced the howling mob, took the cigar from his mouth and shouted, "All right, you guys! Go ahead and hang me, if you wanna, I can't stop you. But lemme tell you, I guarantee that if you hang me, there will be some guys down here from N'Yawk that will blow this here whole dump right off the map!"

Actually, there was probably no one outside his own family who gave a hoot whether Joe was strung up or not. Nevertheless, the threat of reprisal was enough to scare the crowd off for a while, long enough to give manager and fighter the chance to escape with whole skins and the precious light-heavyweight title.

On another occasion, little Joe wandered down to Madame Bey's training camp to watch his featherweight champion, Andre Routis, go through his paces. There he caught sight of an unknown German heavyweight in training. One look was enough. Joe took over the management of the unknown and began to sing his praises. "Fellas," he said confidently, "I got me a heavyweight who looks like Dempsey, so help me, weaves and bobs like Dempsey, he is Dempsey! Or maybe his twin yet. He'll win the title for sure!"

And win it he did, thanks to Joe Jacobs' quick mind. For the unknown German was flat on his back, grovelling in the resin and groaning with pain, when the fast-thinking little man with the cigar leaped up screaming, "Foul! My fighter was fouled!" The referee who had not seen a low blow finally awarded the title to the recumbent fighter on the say-so of one of the judges who claimed to have seen it. Actually, no one but Joe Jacobs had seen the foul deed perpetrated. Fast thinking gave Joe a champion in Max Schmeling, first man in heavyweight history to win a title in a relaxed position on the canvas.

Later, the little character found himself an overstuffed bouncer by the name of Tony Galento. This boisterous clown almost brought Joe another championship with a single blow landed on the face of Joe Louis. Unfortunately for Jacobs, Joe did not stay down. When he did get up, what he did to Two-Ton Tony was pure murder.

A lot of guys in the boxing game did a quick gulp when Joe Jacobs suddenly passed away. They remembered his record as a manager. Five champions did Joe handle: Frankie Genaro, bantamweight champion; Andre Routis, king of the feathers; Jack Delaney and Mike McTigue, light-heavyweight title-holders; and Max Schmeling, heavyweight champion. A grand record for a grand little guy!

AN ODDITY OF THE BOXING GAME IS THE FACT THAT GREAT fighters have so often proved poor managers. For some reason, men seasoned in the ring by scores of hard fights find it impossible to transplant that knowledge into the heads and fists of boxers under their management.

No one will dispute the fact that Sam Langford was a great fighter. He was often called the uncrowned king of the heavyweights. There was nothing the big fellow didn't know about boxing. And no one could hit any harder.

One day old Sam bought himself a piece of another fighter and thus became a manager in partnership with a veteran in the business. Sam's new bruiser made his next fight in the bull ring at Juárez. The fellow in the other corner was a very tough hombre. Sam, in deference to superior experience, let his partner take charge.

After the first round, Sam's partner leaned over the ropes to give advice to his boy, and Sam listened attentively. "Look, kid," said Sam's partner, "you're getting hit with a left hook. Watch out for that punch."

Sam shook his head angrily at the partner. "What do you want to tell him that for?" he demanded. "Don' tell him he's gettin' hit with a left hook, man, when he don' even know about it! Any time a man gets hit with a left hook and he don' know it, then he wants to git plumb out of the boxing business and git hisself a job on a farm!"

After the second round, which had been furiously fought, Sam's partner again began to advise the youngster. "Take it easy, kid," he warned. "You're tired. You're very tired!"

Again old Sam shook his head and contributed his two cents worth. "Man, what for you tell the boy he's tired?" he asked. "If he's tired, don' he know it?"

"You mind your own business!" barked Sam's partner. "I'll do the advising in this fight!"

A short but bitter argument followed on this remark. Finally the partner threw up his hands in disgust and left the arena, abandoning his fighter to the tender mercies of old Sam Langford.

When the fighter returned from the center of the ring at the end of round three, he found only Sam in his corner. The kid was a sight. Sam sponged him off, bathed the cuts, helped him wash out his mouth, but said not a word of advice or otherwise.

At the end of round four, Sam's youngster came back to his corner looking even worse than before. Again Sam cleaned him up and said nothing. With a few seconds to go before the bell for the next round, the kid asked, "Sam, what should I hit him with?"

Sam did not answer. The young fighter repeated the remark. This time there was the sound of pleading in his voice. Old Sam hesitated, then spoke. "Ah'll tell you, sure, boy," he said slowly. The young fighter leaned down, intent to hear the priceless advice that would come from the lips of this most skillful and most feared man in the ring. "Ah'll tell you what to do," went on old Sam, gradually raising his voice, "so listen." And, in a shout that could be heard in all corners of the bull ring, he roared, "Hit him wit' sump'n! Hit him wit' sump'n!"

With this valuable bit of advice to carry him on, Sam's fighter pranced into the center of the ring. There he met a flurry of blows and was knocked cold. Needless to say, so was Sam Langford's career as a manager!

CAULIFLOWER PORTRAITS AND PROFILES

I will remember him as I almost always saw him, standing in a neutral corner of a ring, looking with sleepy-eyed indifference at a prostrate foe. He was the fightingest champion in ring history. For no one ever held the heavyweight title longer, defended it more often or wore the crown with more regal and dignified bearing than Joe Louis.

He defended his title more often than all the other heavyweight champions combined. Twenty-five times he staked his coveted laurels against all comers, white or black. It was unprecedented. Eleven years he remained champion—a record in ring history.

Son of a cotton picker, born in wretched poverty in an Alabama shack, Joe Louis earned a fortune of seven million dollars. It speaks well for democracy that such a story as that of Joe Louis could have happened in America.

When Jack Johnson, first Negro to win the heavyweight championship, hounded by the law and deserted by his own people, finally passed into defeat, the boxing world heaved a deep sigh of relief. When Joe Louis, the second Negro to hold the heavyweight championship of the world retired undefeated, the boxing world heaved a deep sigh of regret. This unlettered pugilist who became king of all fighters was the greatest influence for good boxing ever has had. No pugilist was ever more universally loved, respected and honored than Joe Louis. In the ring, he fought for money and glory, but he never cheapened himself in the quest. Outside the ring, he never failed to create good will among all people. A famous sports reporter once aptly summed up the life and career of Joe Louis in but a few words when he said: "He is a credit to his race—the human race."

Uneducated, nevertheless his tongue always spoke with the simplicity and wisdom of a great man.

When Joe Louis was in the Army during World War II, he was called upon to fight in defense of his heavyweight crown without receiving a single penny for his fistic talents. He contributed his share of the purse to the Army. When the hard-boiled cynics of Cauliflower Alley sneered at his gesture, Joe Louis stilled them with a simple and humble reply:

"I'm not fighting for nothing. I'm fighting for my country."

On the way to the title, the only man to lick Joe was an arrogant and boastful German named Max Schmeling, a former heavyweight champion. Schmeling knocked out Louis in twelve rounds. When Joe Louis became the heavyweight champion of the world, shortly after, he quickly and fearlessly gave Max Schmeling a crack at the million-dollar title. As far as Joe Louis was concerned, it was to be just another prize fight, but Max Schmeling with his boasts of Germanic superiority, built up that fight into an act of nationalism. At the time, Max Schmeling was Adolph Hitler's pet and he craved the heavyweight title to help the mad Hitler verify his claim of Nazi superiority.

Shortly before that international fight, Joe Louis paid a visit to the White House to see a man who had done a great deal for the Negro race. President Franklin Delano Roosevelt turned his famous warm smile on humble Joe Louis. The President of the United States and the simple boy born in an Alabama shack chatted for several minutes in friendly talk. Then Franklin Delano Roosevelt, something of a sportsman himself, felt the fighter's muscles, and said:

"Joe, too many little people want to see you win this fight. Remember, Joe, when the cause is right an American never loses."

"I won't let you down, Mr. President," Joe Louis replied. Joe Louis knocked out Max Schmeling in 2 minutes and 4 seconds of the first round. It was the fastest and most vicious knockout in the history of heavyweight title fights.

There are many stories told about Joe Louis, his greatness as a fighter, his simplicity as a man, his sportsmanship. But I think no story does more justice to the greatness of this humble colored boy than this tale which, curiously enough, has nothing to do with the prize ring.

Not so very long ago, at the height of his career, Joe Louis purchased a large farm near Detroit, a place called Springhill. Springhill was near Utica, Michigan, on the Clinton River. Joe's plan was to turn that dilapidated, broken-down farm into a modern dude ranch, a place to which he could retire when his fistic days were done.

At the time of purchase, and unknown to Joe Louis, there was a long and interesting story associated with that Springhill farm. Springhill had been owned, about a hundred years before, by a man named Peter Lerich. Lerich was a rich man and a great humanitarian. A bitter opponent of slavery, he was a staunch supporter of Abraham Lincoln when the Civil War broke out. To help, he turned his farm into a haven of refuge. Under his roof, runaway slaves found shelter, warmth, food, hope and friendship. Peter Lerich's farm became one of the last stops in the United States on the "underground railway" by which escaped slaves were smuggled into Canada.

With the passing of the years, old Peter Lerich died. His farm fell on evil days. The land was left untilled and

the old buildings became shabby, broken-down and deserted. One day, Joe Louis, searching for a place that he
could use as a training camp and later as a home, came
across the old farm that was now up for sale to the first
bidder. He purchased Springhill.

Soon after, one frosty morning, Joe Louis visited Springhill, mounted a horse, and set out on a tour of inspection
to look over the acres that he had bought. As he was riding
along the river's edge, he saw, about a quarter of a mile
away, a faint column of smoke. He followed the trail and
soon came to a squatter's shack that was hidden in the wil-
lows along the river bank. He rode up to the door and
called out. After a few minutes, an old man, heavily
bent with age, came to the door, followed by his wife.

"Good morning," Joe Louis called out cheerfully. "Do
you folks live here?"

The old man and his wife turned frightened eyes upon
this strange Negro on horseback, but made no reply.

"Kinda cold livin' here these days, isn't it?" asked Joe,
trying to be friendly.

The old man spoke up with a raspy, frightened voice that
still had a touch of pride in it. "Sure, stranger, me and
my wife live in this shack. It's been cold, but it's our only
home. We jes' heard that the farm has been sold to a new
owner and we're skeered that now we'll lose our little
home. It ain't much, stranger, but this shack is our home,
always been our home. I'm the grandson of Peter Lerich
who owned all this land 'bout a hundred years ago and we
jes' can't bear the thought o' leavin' this farm."

Joe Louis looked down at the descendant of the man
who had done so much for his race when they were slaves.
Then he shook his head and said, "Guess there ain't much
chance of you folks being put off this land. I'm the new
owner. Why don't you folks move into the big tenant house

up on the hill? It's warm and dry there and maybe I can fix you up with other things you might be needin'."

That very morning, the old couple moved into the big house up on the hill, the house that had been remodelled as a luxurious home for the great and famous Joe Louis, heavyweight champion of the world. And there the grandson of Peter Lerich has lived ever since without a single worry about rent or keep to embitter his old age.

Joe Louis, oddly enough, never told this story of his kind deed to anyone. When he repaid an ancient debt to Whig Lerich, a forgotten old man whose grandfather one hundred years ago helped to free Negro slaves, he did it without any bluster or pomp.

When all the tales of Joe Louis are told, there will remain but one way to sum up the saga of this great champion:

"He placed a rose on Abe Lincoln's grave."

THIS MIGHT BE CALLED A STORY OF A PRIZE FIGHTER WHO was both a success and a failure. It might also be called a story of a prize fighter who quit the ring to win success in an another field of sports. To me, it's a story of a most amazing man and his courage.

Felix Martinez is a little guy in his late forties. He has always been a little man, short, wiry, and with a big grin carved into his face. But a couple of decades ago, Martinez was a pugnacious two-fisted little battler who had come out of Spain to America to win fame and fortune in the ring. By weight and measure, the little guy was a flyweight.

As such, Felix Martinez became one of the best in the country. Many claimed that he was the best in the world. He went through the flyweight class like a cyclone, licking everyone in his path. With fame and fortune in the palm of his hand, Martinez at last reached the goal of all great fighters—a match with the flyweight champion of the world for the title.

Martinez' big moment came in 1927, the moment he had so long been waiting for. He was sure he couldn't miss winning the title he had so dreamed of winning. Then, in training camp, only a few days before the scheduled title bout, Felix Martinez suffered a slight injury. He didn't tell anyone about it.

The accidental injury cost Martinez the thing he treasured most in life. Not only did he fail to win the title but he took a brutal beating in the process of losing.

Heartbroken, Felix Martinez quit the ring for good. He never fought again.

That was a couple of decades ago, but Felix Martinez did not sink into the obscurity that usually accompanies the man who leaves his chosen profession. He decided to seek fame in some other field of sports. Of all things, Martinez took up fencing. Perhaps he chose the foil and sabre because duelling was the closest thing to fighting with gloves that he could find.

He wasn't satisfied to be just another fencer, though. The ex-prize fighter wanted to be the best in the game! For long and weary hours, for days and weeks and months, Martinez practiced with the foils until he acquired the skill that made him, at last, one of the most feared swordsmen in America.

He has won wide recognition and innumerable bouts in the years that followed his retirement from the ring. The little fellow who might have become a flyweight champion of the world except for an accidental injury just before the bout for the title is a stirring example of courage and grit. And not the least important proof of the courage of the little man is the fact that for more than twenty years now, Felix Martinez has been stone blind.

IF BOXING IS A BIG MONEY SPORT TODAY IT IS BECAUSE ONE man had the vision, the nerve, and the spirit of adventure to make it so. That man was Tex Rickard.

What a colorful and fabulous figure was that long lean bold-eyed gambling man! From the day he left the Lone Star State where he had been an obscure cowhand, he was a restless wanderer in search of adventure. He roamed through the frozen Yukon, the Alaska gold rush, won and lost fortunes in gambling in Nevada, punched cattle in South America.

It was in the Nevada boom town of Goldfield that Tex Rickard became a boxing promoter. At the time he was the owner of a dance and gambling hall. Goldfield was rich and feeling big and important after having taken twenty million dollars in silver and gold out of the ground. The town wanted publicity on a national scale. They turned to Tex Rickard to get it for them.

Rickard was a man of imagination. He knew that the two best fighters in the country at that time were Joe Gans, lightweight champion of the world and Battling Nelson, his bitter rival. There was not a boxing promoter in the country who could tempt the two men to step into the same ring. Rickard, though green at the game, found the answer. He startled the sports world with his daring. He announced that he was offering the two fighters a purse of thirty thousand dollars in gold to meet for the title in Goldfield. No one believed that the match could be made. No one thought that two such famous fighters would be willing to match punches in the middle of a desert.

Everybody was wrong. The Gans-Nelson fight was held in Goldfield, and, what is more, Tex Rickard came out of it with a profit. From then on, Tex was a fight promoter.

Not long after, he again startled the sports world by staging the historic Johnson-Jeffries fight for the heavyweight championship of the world. By now, Tex was really tasting the thrill of big promotions. There was nothing left for him to do but hit the big town. He came on to New York.

It was the match he arranged between Jack Dempsey and the fragile Frenchman, Georges Carpentier, that really made fistic history. The fight drew more than ninety thousand people and took in a gate of one million dollars, the first in history!

Tex Rickard made boxing a respectable sport and big business at the same time. He followed the Dempsey-Carpentier affair with several other million dollar spectacles. To top it all off, he put on the second Dempsey-Tunney fight before one hundred and twenty thousand fight fans. And the gate for the first time went over two million dollars!

Before he died, Tex Rickard built an everlasting monument to his fame as the world's greatest boxing promoter. This was Madison Square Garden in New York, the largest indoor sports arena in the world and the capitol of boxing. Let it never be forgotten that it was Tex Rickard who put the boxing glove into the empire of big business.

USUALLY A PRIZE FIGHTER IS JUST A PUG. HIS CAREER BEGINS and ends inside the ropes. All the glory, all the fame and honor he achieves in life, are bounded by the squared circle. Then, when the last bell sounds and his ring days are done, the ordinary prize fighter, as a subject of news interest, becomes as dead as yesterday's newspaper.

But this story is about Mickey Walker, who was not an ordinary guy in the ring, not a public figure only while he fought, a vague memory after his fighting days were over. Long after his last fight, he is still popping up in the news, each newspaper item about him more incredible than the last.

That Mickey Walker was a first-rate prize fighter no one can deny. About twenty-five years ago, he was feared in fistic circles as the "Toy Bulldog," a sensational ringman who could batter a man to a pulp with two padded mittens laced on his iron fists. That nickname was not just a colorful tag. It really meant something!

Mickey Walker started his ring career with nothing except two swinging fists and a heart of flame. His rise was rapid. It didn't take long before he became welterweight champion of the world.

It wasn't the limit of his ambition, though, to be welter king. Less than four years after he had won that title, Mickey reached up and snagged the middleweight crown. But was that enough! Oh, no! Not while there was a heavyweight title to be fought for!

It was about ten years after he won the welterweight title that Mickey Walker crawled through the ropes to fight Jack Sharkey, at that time heavyweight title-holder. Mickey was a little guy fighting against great odds since he was still a middleweight in height and poundage, meeting a full-sized and redoubtable champion. Still, tough little Mickey Walker, in the twilight of his fistic career, put up such a wild and ferocious battle that he almost won the title!

Walker campaigned for nearly twenty years and earned a fortune of more than a million dollars. Sadly enough, when his fighting days were over, Mickey left the ring with exactly the same amount he had had when he fought his first fight—exactly nothing. He had lived free and easy through all those years and the money had gone out as fast as it had come in.

But did Mickey Walker sink back into obscurity as most fighters were content to do? He did not. He decided, instead, that he would become an artist, a painter of pictures. He had never before picked up a paint brush, nor did he know anything about art. Just the same, and with all his usual confidence, Mickey bought himself some paint brushes, an easel, canvases, and colors. He began to paint. His first efforts were certainly crude but they showed talent. People began to whisper. Before long, Mickey Walker's pictures began to create comment in the world of art. His canvases began to be shown in exhibitions at the galleries. They began to sell, and at fancy prices, too. He received as much as a thousand dollars a picture. The "Toy Bulldog" was back in the public eye. He was famous again!

Even his new career as artist wasn't enough for Mickey Walker. He decided to take a fling at the stage as well! Up he popped as a Broadway actor, and the critics lavished praise on his performance. The fighter turned artist proved to be an actor of talent, too!

Mickey Walker's latest move is once more in the news. Instead of roaming up and down the country as a prize fighter, he has become a lecturer before thousands of people anxious to listen to this curious chap who was not satisfied with one career, or two, or even three. There couldn't be a better subject for one of his own lectures, than the many-sided career of Mickey Walker.

HAD FATE BEEN JUST A LITTLE KINDER TO TOMMY LOUGH- ran, that grand fighter who retired as undefeated light heavyweight champion some years ago, he would have been one of our great heavyweight title-holders as well. But Fate held another destiny, as you will see.

Even as a green youngster, Tommy showed signs of greatness to come. What happened to him just before his very first big bout would have unnerved an older and more experienced battler. His opponent was Jimmy Darcy, a fellow who had come out of the Northwest touted as one of the hardest hitters in the light heavyweight class. Before the fight the two men sat in their respective dressing rooms waiting to be called to the ring. There was only a thin partition between the dressing rooms and only Darcy knew this. Figuring that the green kid was shaking with fear anyhow, Darcy raised his voice as he spoke to his manager. The words he spoke rang clear in Tommy's ears next door. "There's a train to New York at eleven o'clock," Darcy was saying. "I want to catch it. Guess I'll have to make sure and stow away this Loughran kid in the first round. Let's go!"

But Tommy entered the ring unafraid and unaffected by Darcy's psychological attack. He gave the older man the most artistic beating of his life. Darcy hardly laid a glove on Loughran that night. And the world saw the beginning of a boxing career of a man who couldn't be beaten with words, only fists!

At the tender age of nineteen, Tommy was fighting and holding his own against such as Gene Tunney and Harry Greb. In boxing skill, he was superb. His speed was breathtaking, his punching and footwork sharp and dazzling.

One day, still in the early years of his career, Tommy wandered down to the camp of Jack Dempsey where the famed Manassa Mauler was training for a title bout. Young Tommy was invited to put on the gloves with the great man. For three rounds, Tommy Loughran boxed the ears off Jack Dempsey. The champion barely laid a glove on the youngster. When Tommy left the camp, there was a bee buzzing in his bonnet. He would make the heavyweight title his objective in the years ahead.

Tommy soon won the light-heavyweight crown. As titleholder he gave everyone a shot at the championship. No one could lick him, and Tommy eventually retired undefeated.

There was still the old ambition to win the heavyweight

title. Although barely a light heavyweight, Tommy tried but Fate barred the door. For Tommy Loughran fought and licked four heavyweight champions of the world, but never could he win the coveted crown. He always fought them either too early or too late, before or after they held the title.

There was Jack Sharkey, for instance. Tommy licked him before Sharkey won the title. Then Tommy fought and licked Primo Carnera before the latter won the crown. Tommy fought and defeated Jim Braddock, and Braddock in time, too, came on to win the championship. And the fourth was Max Baer to whom Tommy Loughran handed a ten-round beating before Baer became title-holder among the heavyweights.

Never once did Tommy taste the glory that comes to the man who holds the heavyweight crown. Too late or too soon, Fate decreed. And, great as his career was, it never reached the topmost height because Tommy Loughran wasn't lucky.

"A MAN CAN NEVER ESCAPE HIS FATE," SAY THE SEERS, AND so it is, even in the world of sports. No better example of the adage can be found than Eddie Eagan.

During the first World War, Jack Dempsey, great heavyweight champion, came to Denver to put on a boxing exhibition. Into the ring with him was tossed an eager seventeen-year-old, a college kid from Denver University. His name was Eddie Eagan.

To the wild delight of the crowd, the youngster not only went the distance with the great Manassa Mauler, but gave as good as he got all through the battle with the most murderous puncher in boxing history.

After the match, Dempsey threw his arm around the kid's shoulder and said, "Eddie, you're a rugged strong kid. You've got a great future in boxing. Wouldn't surprise me if some day you're the champ!"

Years later, when the great Dempsey was no longer the title-holder, his successor, the United States Marine, Gene Tunney, stepped into the ring in an exhibition against Eddie Eagan. And again after that fight, Tunney said to the young amateur, "Eddie, you're one of the best boxers I've ever fought. You're the greatest amateur fighter I've ever seen. If you were to enter the ring, I'm sure you would wind up as heavyweight champion."

But Eddie Eagan never did become a prize fighter. He went to Yale University and then became a lieutenant of field artillery in World War I. While in Paris with the A.E.F. he won the A.E.F. and Inter-Allied Games middleweight titles.

In 1920, Eddie was back at Yale. There he quickly won recognition as the greatest amateur boxer in the world. He won the National A.A.U. heavyweight title and the same year captured the Olympic light-heavyweight title at Antwerp. In every sense of the word, Eddie Eagan was the "Gentleman Boxer." Promoters and managers stumbled all over each other to sign him up for Eagan looked like a man who couldn't miss winning the heavyweight crown.

However, with the boxing world at his feet, and with all its rich plums his for the taking, Eddie Eagan tossed away boxing fame for books. He entered Harvard Law School, graduated with honors, and won a Rhodes scholarship to study at Oxford University, England. But even at Oxford, Eddie could not quite escape the boxing world. While soaking up more learning, he took enough time off to win the amateur heavyweight championship of the British Empire.

What the world lost as a possible heavyweight boxing champion, the legal world gained as a distinguished lawyer. It seemed that this young man, touted by Dempsey and Tunney, holder of every amateur title, was lost to the boxing world forever. Or so the young man hoped. But remember the adage at the beginning of this story. A man can never escape his fate. After serving with distinction in World War II as lieutenant-colonel in the Air Force, Eddie Eagan was appointed head of the New York State Boxing Commission, probably the most responsible job in the boxing world.

You'd expect the rough and ready world of fisticuffs to resent the appointment of a Yale, Harvard and Oxford man to such a position. But who is more appropriately placed than this man who might have been a boxing champion had he wished?

OF ALL THE STRANGE PERSONALITIES IN SPORTS-LOVING America, One-eyed Connolly was unique. His business consisted merely of crashing the gate at sporting events. One-eyed Connolly made an art of this queer profession. Over the years he wangled his way without payment into more major sports events than any man alive. His persistency always met with success. It got so after a while that One-eyed Connolly, a shabby fellow wearing a dirty cap, had only to appear on the scene of a major sporting event, and the gate would swing wide to let him in. The promoters knew it was no use trying to keep him out. One-eyed would always find the loophole.

It was at championship fights that One-eyed Connolly performed his tricks most skillfully. He never missed in forty years of crashing gates—until the day came when his best wiles were of no avail. It's an amusing story.

One-eyed Connolly showed up in his usual sartorial disrepair to attend a big fight at an outdoor arena in Chicago. For some reason or other, one of the fighters in the main event had taken a violent dislike to One-eyed. There had been some sort of argument between the two, and, to get revenge, the fighter insisted that the promoter take every precaution to keep One-eyed Connolly from getting in without a ticket.

When the word came to One-eyed, he snorted in ridicule. Imagine anyone trying to make him buy a ticket to get in to see a sports event! He'd show them.

When One-eyed showed up in front of the arena on the night of the fight, he whistled. This was really going to be a job. At every gate stood a stalwart minion of the law, ready to give him the bum's rush.

It seemed for a minute that One-eyed Connolly had at last met his Waterloo. The crowds slowly filed into the arena. Hours passed. Still One-eyed Connolly was on the outside. His reputation was ruined, his career lay at his feet in fragments. Time was fast running out. Inside, the main event had already started. Something had to be done, and fast.

Suddenly, inside the arena, a brick came sailing from over the low fence and landed right in the middle of the ring where the two fighters were busily mixing it.

The frightened referee looked at the brick for a moment, then picked it up. Ignoring the fighters completely, he stepped to the side of the ring. Leaning far over the ropes, he shouted to the ticket taker standing guard at the main gate in a voice that could be heard for miles. "Hey, you! Open up that gate and let One-eyed Connolly in! He's outside! I know, because he just sent in his card!"

One-eyed Connolly entered in triumph, his record still intact, his reputation as the world's greatest gate-crasher untarnished!

HEAVYWEIGHT FIGHTS MAY COME AND GO BUT I DOUBT whether there will ever be another quite like the one in which Luis Firpo, Wild Bull of the Pampas, came within one second of winning the crown.

Luis Firpo was a big, hairy, powerful hunk of man who had been a bottle washer in his native Buenos Aires before deciding to become a fighter. He arrived in New York on a slow tramp steamer, a paper suitcase in one hand, and in the other a hat too small for his head. He did not know a single boxing promoter in the States. Nevertheless, in two years, Luis Firpo had battled his way to a crack at the heavyweight championship of the world.

He was no fancy Dan. He didn't know a thing about boxing, but he had a punch, a paralyzing punch that had laid low every heavyweight they tossed into the ring with him. When they finally sent him into the ring against the champion, Jack Dempsey, the man reputed to be the most savage heavyweight of them all, ninety thousand spectators were there to see the Wild Bull of the Pampas make his challenge.

The bell clanged. The two men charged towards each other. The first punch was thrown. It was the crude, hard-hitting Firpo who landed it and the crowd rose hysterically to its feet. The great Jack Dempsey was on the floor.

The Manassa Mauler jumped back to his feet and flung a terrific blow to Firpo's jaw. The huge South American dropped to the canvas like a stricken bull. Glowering and tense, Dempsey stood over the man from the Argentine, right fist cocked for another punch. Firpo's knees were hardly clear of the floor when Dempsey hit him again. Six or seven times was the giant Firpo knocked down. To this day no one knows exactly how often it was, but each time the giant South American climbed gamely to his feet to take all the champion could dish out.

On his seventh trip up from the canvas, Firpo made a wild and desperate rush at Dempsey, driving the champion across the ring. Near the ropes, Firpo fired one last haymaker which lofted Dempsey completely out of the ring and into the laps of the first row of spectators. It was the supreme moment of Firpo's life. He was just ten seconds away from the title and the million dollars that would go with it.

But the referee never counted those ten seconds. He just stood there dumbfounded. Willing hands pushed Jack Dempsey back into the ring. The round ended. Firpo's big chance was over. He was knocked out in the second round.

After the battle, Firpo came into Dempsey's dressing room. "How are you, kid?" shouted Dempsey.

"I, Señor Dempsey, am fine," replied Firpo proudly. "I can only say that you do not look as well and that I should be the heavyweight champion of the world. I go back to Buenos Aires. I will be a beeg man there now, señor. All I wanted was to beat you." And he turned on his heel and slammed the door shut behind him.

Luis Firpo never achieved his ambition to lick the champion but luck in other ways rode with him from that time on. According to the latest reports, the former Wild Bull of the Pampas has become a South American motion pic-

ture magnate, with a fortune reputed to be as high as seven million dollars!

THE DAY PRIMO CARNERA SLIPPED OUT OF THIS COUNTRY TO return to his native Italy, people laughed, shook their heads, and promptly forgot the awkward simpleton's comic opera career as a fighter. Primo, a sadder and wiser man than he had been when he first arrived in America, had nothing but a little house in his native Sequals, Italy, to show for his million dollars of earnings as a fighter.

Primo Carnera was an unknown circus roustabout in Paris some twenty years ago when he was invited to take part in a prize fight by Mississippi-born Jeff Davis Dickson in the *Salle Wagram*. Every one whistled in astonishment at his size and proportions, but he was knocked out ignominiously in two rounds. Carnera should have been promptly forgotten as an awkward and clumsy clown. But there was one man in the audience who had watched the big fellow's lumbering endeavours and this man was a shrewd little manager named Leon See. He took the big Italian under his wing, to start one of the most amazing careers in boxing history.

Carnera was brought to America. In some way, he picked up managers as sugar picks up flies. He soon had half-a-dozen of them and his earnings were being cut more ways than an apple pie in a boarding house.

Primo's managers, who had spent more time in prisons than the tiger-toothed giant had spent on earth, fixed up a series of fixed bouts. They made sure the big boy could not lose by making business-like arrangements beforehand, sometimes through persuasion, often enough by means of threats and a show of force. Through all this Carnera went his simple way, never knowing that he was meeting stumble-bums, tankers, and diving specialists.

The public was aware that most of the bouts that Carnera fought were from Gorgonzola. But the public made at least one mistake.

Primo was matched to fight a heavyweight of promise named Ernie Schaaf. The six-foot seven-inch 270-pound giant towered over his opponent in the ring. The whisper was out that the fight was another one of those boat-rides. When Schaaf dropped to the canvas from what most spectators thought was a light jab, howls of rage went up.

Even as the fight fans were yelling "Fake!", Ernie Schaaf was being carried to the hospital in an unconscious state. And the debate was still raging a few days later when the electrifying news came from the hospital that Schaaf was dead. An autopsy revealed that he had died of a brain injury.

Ironically enough, it was only now that Carnera began to be taken seriously. He was finally matched for the world's heavyweight title.

What a surprise that fight turned out to be! Ponderous, clumsy Primo Carnera, the man who had been built up on the basis of a phony reputation, turned in a splendid exhibition of skill and punching power as he outfought, outsmarted and outboxed clever Jack Sharkey for the coveted crown.

It was Carnera's supreme moment as a prize fighter. Soon after, the Amiable Alp was slaughtered in the ring by the magnificent playboy heavyweight, Maxie Baer.

His fighting days at an end, Primo Carnera began to count the profits of his meteoric career. He found it unnecessary to use more than the fingers of his right hand to reach the total. He had earned a million dollars in the ring. Not a dime remained to him. His managers had cleaned him thoroughly.

Broke, bewildered and beaten, Primo Carnera left these

hospitable shores for his native Italy. He was forgotten—
but not for good.

News about the big fellow came through from time to
time. During the war, the man who had made a million
was working for fifteen cents a day swinging pick and
shovel for the Nazis in his home town. Everybody felt
sorry for the friendly giant but there were more serious
things to think about in those days.

Now? Oh, things are all different now. Primo Carnera
is well on his way to another million bucks. What's more,
he is well on his way to being an American citizen—yes,
he came back all right—owns a big home in Los Angeles,
a fat bank account that is growing by leaps and bounds,
and the same friendly snag-toothed smile. How come?
Primo Carnera has joined the fraternity of Burp, Grunt
and Growl. He is a wrestler, a professional wrestler, and
his bouts draw them by the thousands. It doesn't matter
that the bouts are just exhibitions and there are hundreds
of honest amateurs who could toss Primo over their shoulders into the next county. There's plenty of gold in those
grunts—and Primo's keeping it all!

When the magic words "Boxing Tonight" light up on
the marquee of world-famed Madison Square Garden in
New York, thousands of fight fans come pouring into the
broad lobby in eager quest of tickets. They know that only
the greatest, the best fighters are allowed to display their
wares in that arena. I have gone there just as eagerly as any
other fan, but I never failed to see, as so many others did, a
certain little man, no bigger than a welterweight, who
lolled carelessly against the wall of the lobby, watching the
crowds. To my mind, he was the greatest two-fisted fighter
that ever lived though he never appeared in the ring. His
name is Johnny Broderick. This is just a little of his story.

Johnny Broderick was a member of the New York police force, a detective in plain clothes. The toughest gangsters feared Johnny and avoided him like the plague. And yet, Johnny never used a club or a blackjack or a gun. It was with his bare fists that Johnny maintained law and order. And how that little man could sock! The toughest mobsters found it advisable to walk around the block when Johnny hove into view. There wasn't a man he couldn't lick in a rough-and-tumble fight. Only a few hard guys tried conclusions with the little terror, once his reputation was established. A couple of such instances come quickly to mind.

One night, some time ago, an important fight was staged in the Garden. As the thousands poured into the lobby and through the gates to the arena, Detective Johnny Broderick leaned casually against a post surveying the scene. Suddenly, pushing their way through the crowd came a notorious mobster chief with his six tough bodyguards. The mobster was Vannie Higgins, a guy feared all over the country. So far he had evaded the clutches of the law which had not yet managed to get the goods on him. As he was about to step through the gate, Johnny left his post and came to the gangster's side.

"You're not wanted in here tonight, Vannie," said Broderick. "Don't come in."

The gang chief sneered. "What's eating you, flatfoot?" he snarled. "I've got a ticket."

Johnny grinned gently in reply. "Ticket or no ticket," he said softly, "don't come in. Your bodyguards can come in, but not you. If you step across the door sill, I'll have to flatten you."

Vannie considered the situation. Why should he be afraid of this little cuss? He could chew up a dozen like him!

"Don't annoy me, copper," he said at last. "I got a fight to see."

He stepped back a little to let his bodyguards precede him into the arena. Smirking and sneering, the six men came through the door. Then the chief started to follow them. No sooner had he stepped across the sill than Johnny Broderick threw a left hook that folded the gang leader across the ticket-taker's booth. The gangster chief crawled to his feet and lunged at the detective. Broderick hit him with a right hand that lifted him clean off the floor and dumped him again. Then Johnny leaned down casually, grabbed the battered gunman chief by his gaudy necktie and dragged him to a corner.

"Get up, you yellow bum!" ordered Johnny. The groggy mobster climbed slowly to his feet. Broderick chucked a terrific right hand punch that slammed the gangster right through the glass-panelled doors of the phone booths in the lobby. Leaving the fallen mobster where he was, Broderick walked up to the now cringing bodyguards and snapped, "Now, all of you get out of here! I'd have had some respect for you if you had tried to help your boss, but you yellow bums are no good! What's he paying you for anyway? Get out, before I go to work on all of you!"

The six toughies scurried away from there in a hurry. Johnny Broderick once again grabbed the gang boss, pulled him out of the lobby and tossed him into the gutter of Eighth Avenue! Then, as though nothing unusual had happened, he returned to his leaning post in the lobby and again began to watch the crowd pouring into the Garden for the fight they had come to see. They couldn't have seen a better fight that night than the one that had taken place in the lobby!

No matter where they were, or what they were doing, the hoodlums used to make tracks whenever Johnny Broderick appeared on the scene. Any time there was a sudden scramble for the exits, be it in a night club or a restaurant along the Great White Way, it was usually the signal that Johnny Broderick had come to look over the situation. A lot of people would stop breathing until Johnny, satisfied that the bad boys were behaving, went away.

But not all the tough guys were smart enough to keep under cover when Johnny was looking for them. One of the most savage of the hoodlums, a mug whose reputation for viciousness was tops even among the mobsters, was dining in a Broadway eating place when Johnny came looking for him. The detective caught sight of him immediately and crossed the room.

"You're my boy, Pretty," he said quietly. Then Johnny, without another word, dragged the burly mobster out of the restaurant to the street. One blow to the mid-section bent the mobster double. Standing there, his head down and his rear end up, Pretty Amberg was an inviting target. Johnny Broderick stepped back. Contemptuously, he let fly with the toe of his foot and kicked the hoodlum head first through the plate glass window of the store next to the restaurant. Johnny followed him through the jagged opening, grabbed him by the hair of the head, and dragged him to the curb where a police car waited for Johnny to deliver his prisoner.

That's the sort of man Johnny Broderick was, the most dreaded cop in the city of New York. The mobsters feared him because he was not afraid of them, and because he let them have it in full view of everybody, in the open streets where their humiliation would be plain to see.

Johnny Broderick is in Hollywood now, living a peaceful and tranquil life. But no matter how far-off he gets, and how quietly he lives, Boxing Row will never forget Johnny Broderick, the man who never fought in the ring, but who was the best two-fisted fighter that ever threw a punch.

A SELECTED LIST OF

GENUINE **POCKET** BOOK EDITIONS